PATRIOT FOR LIBERTY

TO THEE OLD CAUSE!
THOU PEERLESS, PASSIONATE, GOOD CAUSE,
THOU STERN, REMORSELESS, SWEET IDEA,
DEATHLESS THROUGHOUT THE AGES, RACES, LANDS . . .

—WALT WHITMAN

PATRIOT FOR LIBERTY

Leon Solomon White

J. B. LIPPINCOTT COMPANY

PHILADELPHIA AND NEW YORK

U.S. Library of Congress Cataloging in Publication Data

White, Leon Solomon, birth date
  Patriot for liberty.

  SUMMARY: Follows the adventures of a young New Yorker during the time
between the Boston Tea Party and the reading of the Declaration of
Independence.
  1. United States—History—Revolution, 1775–1783—Causes—Juvenile
fiction. [1. United States—History—Revolution, 1775–1783—Causes—Fic-
tion] I. Title.
PZ7.W5838Pat   [Fic]   74-30451
ISBN-0-397-31619-4

For Paula

N

HUDSON RIVER

Lispenard Mansion

Road to Greenwich

Fresh Water Pond

Warren Street

Common

Dyes Street

8

George Street

Prince Street

Queen Street

Ann Street

John Street

Cherry Street

Water Street

6

5

Broadway

Wall Street

Queen Street

Beekman's slip

Peck's slip

Broad Street

3

Dock Street

Rootman's slip

2

Murray's Wharf

The Battery

4

Whitehall slip

EAST RIVER

A.M. JAUSS

Road to Boston

Bowery Lane

Crista

Delancy's Square

Street

RopeWalk ---- Division Street

Yards

Crown Pt. or Corlar's Hook

NEW YORK CITY

1. Fort George   7. Hull's
2. The Bowling Green   8. St. Paul's
3. Customs House   9. Hampden Hall
4. The Exchange   10. The Liberty Pole
5. The City Hall   11. Montagnie's
6. Trinity

— After the Bernard Ratzer map of 1767 —

1.

December 1773

WE WERE CONVENED in meeting in the upstairs chamber of
Montagnie's, sitting as the Committee of Inspection and
listening to one of Counselor Dinwiddie's hypocritical and
tiresome perorations, when through the partly open window
that vented our crowded fervors and disagreements and
above the murmur of the ordinary sounds of the town in late
afternoon there came the drumming of horses' hooves on
the gallop down Broadway.

Being openly opposed to the speaker, both in his views
and in his character, I felt privileged to shift my attention to
the more novel noise outside. I turned in my chair and
looked down into the street—barely in time to see Revere of
Boston race past.

I motioned one of the youngsters to me and sent him off
to Hampden Hall, whither the horseman would be bound,
to bring him to the committee. My heart leapt with
expectation even as I did so, for Massachusetts Bay would
not send its chief express rider on an unrelayed journey
clear to New York over a trifle.

On a slip of paper I wrote "Revere has come" and pushed

it to the man beside me. The note passed from one to another of the twenty or so committee members around the long table. Dinwiddie paused to look at it and then went on with his speech—but a trifle more hollowly, it seemed to me. Nor was I the only one to receive that impression. Across from me and several places farther along, Martin Kluger gazed up at the orator with the faintest quizzical lift of his shaggy, graying eyebrows, after which his eyes sought mine and opened a little wider with quiet humor.

I nodded in return and marked to myself how this was the second or third time, recently, that Kluger had singled me out for an expression of his opinion. It was unusual on two accounts: he was a man well into his fifties, whereas I was but a youth, to him, of twenty-two; and our politics were quite at odds.

Dinwiddie had scarcely begun bringing to a conclusion his legalistic embroidery work of analogies and precedents, all properly interwoven with fervent protestations of devotion to His Most Gracious Majesty, when we heard the clattering of hooves returning up the street. A moment later the stairs were creaking to a bouncing pace and Revere himself came striding into the room.

"We are honored!" exclaimed portly old Rutherford, our chairman, rising in his ceremonious manner and taking the rider's hands. "Thomas!" he called to one of the boys. "A chair here for Mr. Revere. And a cup of rum!"

"Thank ye, gentlemen," the stocky New Englander replied. "I have ridden these two hundred and fifty miles from Boston with only the briefest stops to change horses. A cup of rum is welcome indeed!"

Which could readily be believed. I had never before seen him so coated with mud or drenched with perspiration. His open, confident features, almost always aglow with likeable zest, were this time drawn by strain.

"And, Thomas," Rutherford said as the boy stood by, staring with unabashed fascination at the drinking New Englander, "go downstairs and tell Madame Montagnie we'll want her best hot dinner and a room made ready immediately for a friend who has just come a long journey."

"Your dinner will be most welcome, gentlemen, but further hospitality I must refuse. I am to carry my dispatches as far as Philadelphia as quickly as I am able."

Rutherford indicated the chair that had been placed behind him, but Revere continued to stand. Something vibrated within the fatigued yet excited figure that would not permit him to sit down.

"Gentlemen," he announced, "I bring you the greeting of the Boston Committee of Correspondence. I am charged by them to inform you that four evenings ago, after nearly two weeks of counsel-taking among the inhabitants of Boston, gathered over that period in continual town meeting; after much prayer to prepare the conscience, and earnest beseeching of the Most High for guidance; it was determined that the tea aboard the ships which had arrived from England as part of the new taxation scheme must under no circumstances be landed on these shores. Upon the governor's refusal to grant the ships a clearance to leave the harbor unless the tea were first unloaded, and this despite repeated applications from the masters of the ships for such clearance, and despite similar importunities from the consignees, who no longer wished to receive the tea; and upon the governor's determination to make a trial of strength over the landing of the tea, the town meeting dissolved itself; and immediately thereafter a band of unknown men wearing the apparel of Mohawk Indians boarded the three tea-bearing vessels, seized the three hundred and forty-two chests therein, and emptied the tea into Boston Harbor. In which no other item of cargo or equipment was so much as scratched nor was any man in any other way injured or inconvenienced."

Revere paused, and it seemed he might sit down from exhaustion. My own heart was pounding loud and hard against my ribs. The express rider remained standing, however, and after a moment he went on.

"I bear with me a letter from the Boston Committee of Correspondence which I am instructed to read to you, and after which I am to answer your questions and make such further explanations as you may wish and as I am able to supply."

He drew an envelope from an inner pocket and took from it a paper. But before he finished unfolding his letter an uproar broke out in the chamber.

"Rebellion! Open rebellion! The hotheads have over-played their hand!"

"Irresponsibles are committing us to warfare!"

"All we have tried to avoid has come to pass!"

"Oh, that Sam Adams were here! If only we had some way of discussing matters directly with those villains Adams and Hancock!"

Accusations and denunciations and table-slappings filled the room.

Across Revere's face surprise and consternation succeeded each other. His gaze went up and down the table from one expostulating figure to another. Then his full underjaw came forward in anger. Through the tumult he addressed himself to me.

"Were it not for your own presence here, Jamie Hardy, and one or two other faces familiar to me, I should think I had come upon a meeting of your governor's council. Pray, sir, enlighten me."

I rose without waiting for the chairman.

"On behalf of the Sons of Liberty of New York, whose representative I am on this committee, I offer you an apology. Your glorious news deserves a reception far different from this. This gathering is a session of the New York Committee of Inspection, and not, as you may have been led by accident of circumstances to think, of the Sons of Liberty. This committee has been recently established, as you will understand, to bind together in action all shades of opinion that find common ground so far only on one point—to discourage the sale in this colony of English-taxed goods. Since we are all of us patriots, or so profess to be, I had you directed here when I glimpsed you riding past to Hampden Hall, where you would have found no one at this hour. Tonight, however, at the Hall, there will be a regular meeting of the committee of the Sons of Liberty, to whom, if I mistake not, your dispatch is more truly addressed. I beg you to avail yourself of the hospitality proffered you at this inn until eight o'clock, when I will call for you here, myself, and conduct you to that meeting."

Revere replied, "I may not wait to deliver my message to my good friends in person. It is enough, Hardy, that you have heard my news. You will please communicate it yourself to your devoted colleagues."

"Indeed I will," I returned, "and further, I believe I can promise you that by this same time tomorrow the adherents of the Sons of Liberty will be parading our streets and beating their drums in celebration of Boston's inspiring action. And who can tell—" and here I looked round at the roomful of indignant and alarmed cavilers—"who can tell but that we of New York may find Boston's example the proper solution to our own approaching tea problem."

Revere made a short bow with his head. Returning his letter to his pocket he said civilly enough to the others, "Gentlemen, with your leave I will retire."

The moment the express rider left, guided by one of the boys, the room boiled over in intense and aggrieved consultations. In vain, old Rutherford rapped his gavel to bring the meeting back to its regular business. He asked, at last, for a motion to terminate, and then the discussions buzzed on untrammeled.

I myself, hard put to it to master my excitement, wrote out notes to the other members of the Sons of Liberty committee informing them of Boston's action. And sending the notes off with little Thomas, I took my coat from the wall, as it seemed to me that small profit would accrue to the patriot cause if I stayed listening to the lamentations around me.

"Mr. Hardy!"

I turned at the head of the staircase. Martin Kluger was standing beside me, his coat, too, in his hands. In his strong, lined face his small eyes were twinkling. "You do not appear despondent over the news."

"George the Third may be despondent over it, not I."

The little eyes, gray and clear, twinkled even more. "Mr. Hardy, I wonder if you would spare me a portion of your time. The signs indicate dirty weather ahead and I feel it behooves some of us in the ship to become better acquainted with one another."

"I am at your service," I replied.

14

"Please do me the favor of dining with me this evening at my house."

I hesitated. A man in politics who exercises some influence over a following must be careful about which doors he is seen going in and out of. While Martin Kluger's sympathies were well known to be with the patriots, he was also one of the wealthiest ship owners in the town—whereas the following of the Sons counted largely shipwrights, seamen, mechanics, small tradespeople, and the like.

"I fear that the dispositions for dinner you have most probably already made will prove inconvenient for us tonight. I would have to dine and depart early enough to meet with the Sons committee."

"New dispositions can easily be made, sir," Kluger replied. "I have no other guests this evening, which is itself unusual and a good omen for greater understanding between us. And it is that upon which I have set my heart."

"Your servant, sir," I assented.

2.

THE KEEN DECEMBER AIR gave vigor to our pace and it took us little more than fifteen minutes to traverse the length of the town down to the Bowling Green. Here, at the southernmost tip of the island, where the fine houses stood facing one another around the circular little park, we turned in at a pair of tall, intricately worked iron gates.

"Louisa," Kluger addressed the servant who opened the door, "tell Miss Elisabeth we must have dinner earlier than planned—in fact, by half past six. And that there will be one guest."

"Really, now, Father, this is too barbarous! How can you possibly expect a dinner that was intended for half past eight to be served at half past six! And without notice!"

The clear, feminine voice, most pleasantly modulated and musical despite its indignation, came from somewhere above us.

I looked around. We were in a large entrance hall-way with a high ceiling. Midway up the walls a white-balustraded gallery ran round the room, and from this there descended a broad staircase. The voice belonged to a girl who was standing on the gallery near the head of the stairs.

"I'm afraid it would be even more barbarous not to serve dinner at half past six, my dear, as that is when I have promised it to Mr. Hardy, here. It is, in fact, the main condition upon which I have enticed him to our house."

The girl came down the staircase, stepping lightly, yet with dignity.

Kluger presented me. "Elisabeth, this is Mr. James Hardy, a young colleague of mine on the Committee of Inspection." I bowed. "Mr. Hardy, my daughter Elisabeth, who has lately returned from her aunt's, in England, and who finds much in our poor land that is primitive."

She was a striking-looking young lady with a fine, oval face and serious, dark eyes.

"You'll excuse my outburst, I hope, Mr. Hardy," she said, curtseying and ignoring Kluger's comment. "Father is forever making unexpected and almost impossible rearrangements of this sort. Louisa, take Mr. Hardy's coat."

I became oddly aware of the details of my mechanic's workaday dress as I gave my coat to the servant. In this high-ceilinged room with its great staircase and rich hangings, and in the presence of this girl so prettily arrayed in European clothes, I stood in scuffed and turned work boots, patched and stained trousers tucked in at the bottoms and reinforced at the knees with great squares of wadding, loosening a heavy vest designed more for warmth than adornment, and thus displaying my mechanic's shirt, once evenly blue but now whitening and fraying along the edges and seams.

The servant showed me to a closet, where I washed, and then to a large drawing room where Kluger was waiting for me. He was seated to one side of a new fire that crackled on the hearth, beside a small round table bearing a decanter and wineglasses.

He indicated a chair to the other side of the table. "Sherry, sir? It is the finest Spain boasts. I bring it in in my own ships." He smiled grimly. "Carried on the cockets as duly reshipped from our West Indies, of course."

"I do wish you gentlemen would learn to manage your affairs with less haste!"

Miss Kluger had come into the room.

"As the English manage their affairs, no doubt," said her father.

Kluger and I rose and waited till she seated herself on a sofa opposite us on the other side of the fireplace.

"Perhaps. My father thinks I have returned from England filled with disdain for everything in our own colony, Mr. Hardy, but that is not true. I have simply tried to show him ways in which the English do things that appear to me to add to the charm of living."

Her voice was low, light, and pleasant.

"I believe I got her back here barely in time," said Kluger, obviously enjoying twitting her. "Another year and she would not have been able to tolerate at all the rusticities of our land of wigwams and forests."

The girl replied by tilting her head in wordless hauteur. It was a gesture she could make to good effect, for her high cheekbones and delicate profile were in themselves arresting. What really distinguished her, however, from so many other well-cared-for daughters of wealthy families, were her eyes. Under serene brows they were glowing, quick, and complex.

"Apparently you found England interesting," I said.

"Oh, very! The splendid houses there, the castles and the

estates for countryside living, and the marvelously appointed residences in London make a different world from this one. And life there moves at such a proportioned pace!"

I judged her to be about nineteen or twenty, only two or three years younger than myself, an age when brocades and gilt and retinues of servants and elaborate social amusements might make their strongest impressions.

In the interest of civility I said only, "I have often wished I could visit England. Did you attend any sittings of Parliament?"

"It never occurred to me to push in amongst all that pipe-smoking crowd. But I do believe that I saw as much of the government as one could wish. I have seen the Earl of Sandwich come from his office in the Admiralty and devote himself as wholeheartedly as anyone to making a ball go successfully. And I have met Lord North, too, at parties. He is the most darling, amiable, oversized sort of man, with the nicest sense of humor."

"All the same," I said, "I should have liked to hear Charles James Fox make a speech in Parliament. Or Colonel Barre. Even the reports in the papers are stirring."

"Why do you say 'should have liked,' Mr. Hardy? A five weeks' passage over the Atlantic will set you down in London at any time."

"I am too taken up with events just now to leave on a holiday. And should these events take a course they very well might, some of us would not be overly welcome to His Majesty's officers. We have received news only within the hour, for example, that our Boston friends have sent several shiploads of His Majesty's taxed tea into the waters of Boston harbor."

"Disgraceful!" she exclaimed. And having utterly failed

to understand the significance of the act, she rose and said, "Shall we go in to dinner?"

In spite of the disruption of their dinner plans, the table in the room to which we passed seemed to be set as lavishly as for a banquet. The chamber itself was even larger than the one in which we had been sitting, and its cream-colored walls, whose paneling appeared to be worked in gold paint, were draped with heavy, richly colored cloths and hung with portraits. The whole was bathed in light from three large chandeliers.

The regular dinner table, a long affair that stood at one end and extended the width of the room, was not now to be used. It remained undraped and gleaming darkly, and still bore its ornamental silver candlesticks and fruit bowls. Instead, near one of the tall windows, a smaller, round table waited, smothered in damask and napkins and laden with silverware, china, decanters, cruets, and other porcelain, silver, and gold utensils.

Two menservants in livery pushed our chairs under us as we sat down, and thereafter one poured the wines and served the courses and the other removed the dishes. After the fowl had been served, Kluger broached the topic in the forefront of our thoughts.

"Hardy, the English won't merely wink at Boston's tea dumping, you understand."

"I understand that well enough to consider proposing at the Sons meeting tonight that we in New York begin gathering arms and powder and organizing military formations."

I must have caught him unprepared. He paused, his fist with the fork in it dropping back to the table. Finally he said, "You are so ready to fight?"

"If it comes to it."

"And you think it will?"

"It may."

He paused again. "Let me hear why you think so."

"Why, sir, it is the intention of the English, first and always, to exploit the wealth of this continent for themselves. On this policy England's commercial classes and her nobility are united, and to this end they will press a determined course, regardless of the few kind and generous speeches made on our behalf in Parliament by the handful of Barres and Burkes. The whole dispute about these taxes, for example, as I am sure you understand, is nothing other than a struggle to determine who shall hold the purse strings over our governors and our judges—we, who would protect ourselves thereby, or the king and Parliament, acting for the lords and merchants of England, who would control the colonial governments the more easily to rob us."

"For a young man you see things surprisingly as they are," said Kluger.

"I take it then you agree with me?"

He nodded. "Yet not necessarily do I believe we will have to fight—a belief which may engender a rashness of attitude and a forwardness in action that might of themselves evoke armed conflict. Don't you think that, were the colonies to unite and present a peaceable but sufficiently firm opposition, we would convince London their course cannot be successful?"

"I hope so," I replied. "Yet I am not willing to chance too much on that contingency alone. The example of Ireland shows that if one must defend oneself against the English, the time to do so is before they have one by the throat, not after."

The mention of that tortured land added an unexpectedly grim argument to my view. Kluger and I fell into a thoughtful silence.

The first to speak thereafter was the young lady.

"You sound so very strongly opposed to the English, Mr. Hardy. Almost as though they had done you a personal injury. I'm sure that if you knew them better you would find they are not all ogres."

"It is not England to which I am opposed, Miss Kluger, but to all Europe and its feudalism. There are those of us who have engaged ourselves in this dispute not so much over questions of taxation as in the hope of staying the hand of European feudalism from fastening itself upon this new land. We see the record of history clearly enough—that patents of nobility and the pomp and glitter of privilege find their sustenance in an enslaved peasantry and an exhausted artisan class. From one end of old Europe to the other it is all the same ages-old tragic story. We would try, if we can, to bring forth in this new land a happier state of society."

I stopped. I was saying more than I intended for ears in this house. Something in the atmosphere had tricked me into giving expression to ideas I usually kept guarded and close at the very core of my thinking.

But neither of the others sensed this reaction of mine. Kluger was gazing at me in a reflective, abstracted manner. And the girl was searching my eyes with surprising intentness. I was struck all at once with one of those insights we sometimes get into the personality of others and which seem so irrelevant to the circumstances in which they occur. Within her somber, quick eyes I thought I saw a lack of real ease in life and an intensity beyond the usual.

"Where do you get such thoughts?" she said. "I have never heard anyone speak so."

"They are not original with me. John Locke and Rousseau and Voltaire and Montesquieu, to name but a few, have proclaimed them for a hundred years. And the truths they assert are becoming increasingly evident to all who view the affairs of men rationally."

Concern appeared in her eyes. "But you would be destroying the organization of society. People would not know who they really are or what they are supposed to do. The titled nobility directs affairs because it is the class that knows how to do so."

"Not all of us believe that fairy tale. Some of us would try and see whether it is possible to raise up communities in which all of the citizens help to shape policy, and do so for the benefit of all, not for a few."

I stopped. Again I was saying more than I intended. And as I realized why—I was trying to convert this pretty and pampered young lady—I grew warm under my collar and I felt sure some crimson was entering my face. But, again, no one appeared to notice.

Out of the reflectiveness in which he still seemed enwrapped Kluger said to me, "Hardy, how old are you?"

"Twenty-two, sir."

"It is some four months now that I have been associated with you on the Committee of Inspection, and in that brief period I have developed a high regard for you. From my experience with people it seems to me quite probable that two or three years from now—perhaps a little later in your case, for you appear to be a true, stubborn descendant of your Roundhead ancestors—your interests may take a somewhat more personal turn. Your absorption in the welfare of your fellow men may diminish somewhat—by no means disappear, of course—and develop in what you might now consider a more selfish direction. I want you to know that I shall be most happy at that time to have your assistance in my enterprises and I will be most gratified at the opportunity to help you further any of your own plans."

There I had it! Here was the real reason Kluger wanted to speak to me in private. I was being offered a bribe!

To what end?

Boston's tea dumping might well be taken by the Sons of Liberty of New York as a signal for similar action. I had said as much at the meeting. Kluger wanted to buy my influence against such a move. And, for the longer period, he wanted me to be a party to his own attitudes.

"Thank you for what I fear is too flattering an estimate of myself," I replied as evenly as I could. "As for your offer of future assistance, why, thank you again. Should my personal or 'selfish' motivations take too strong a turn, however, I don't believe I should stand very high in my own regard. I don't like to contemplate the prospect."

"No offense, Hardy," Kluger replied. "Your capability is high, I repeat, but you're still quite young—with many more years before you and many more changes of interest possible than a young man imagines. It may well turn out that at some time in the future you will want to take advantage of my aid."

The old fox was covering his tracks now, and doing it ever so well! No one else hearing the conversation could possibly realize what had really been offered in it and rejected. Perhaps with only half a year's less experience in politics I would have had doubts about it all myself.

24

I pushed back my chair. "I thank you for a splendid dinner and a most interesting exchange of views, but I fear I can delay leaving no longer."

Kluger and the girl stood in the hallway with me as I wound on my shawl and put on my coat.

"I'm sorry your visit is so brief," Kluger said. "You must come again. I shall see you next week, of course, this same day, at the Committee of Inspection."

"Please do come again, Mr. Hardy," the girl said.

I had been in the society of wealthy and mannered people before this and had been struck by the dexterity with which they employed the phraseology of courtesy. And yet, aware of it as I was, I found myself searching for something more than the mere form in her few gracious words of goodbye.

Outside the gates I turned north and walked rapidly.

I speculated on how quickly the Sons might yet distribute a notice in what remained of this night, calling on the town to gather at the Common tomorrow to show our brotherhood with Boston; and I wondered mightily about Kluger's surprising effort to bribe me. Yet each phase of my reflections ended with an image of dark eyes in a fine oval face.

There is an unhappiness, or an unease, which comes to each young man and young woman in the course of nature's development and which finds its resolution in marriage. But the intensity, the hints of bafflement, perhaps even moments of private despair, that I thought I read in those deep eyes seemed to me to stem from something more, something that might not find so direct a remedy. It only added to the poignancy that they were so well contained within the thoroughly schooled facade she presented to the world at large.

I almost strode past Hampden Hall in dwelling upon these matters.

3.

THE SUN SHONE bright and steady out of a clear winter sky, taking the harsher edges off the cold December morning. It was excellent weather for a gathering of the citizenry; and to judge by the spirit of the men in the shipyard, the public assembly for which the Sons had called gave promise of turning out a rouser.

Many of the mechanics had come to work carrying the handbill we had slipped under their doors during the night. All through the morning, while the hammering and fitting suffered neglect, they collected in excited groups to surmise and to argue.

At half past eleven, as the sun moved away from the wind-whipped waters of the East River and stood above the masts of the shipyard, I climbed down from a perch where I was overseeing the jointing of a rib into a keel. I rolled a nail keg out into a clear space among the hoists and timbers and mounted upon it.

"Free citizens of New York and mechanics who labor in this shipyard," I announced. "You have all been apprised by now of the action of brave Boston with respect to the loathsome taxed tea and it is plain from your demeanor you understand its import well!"

The clatter of tools began to cease, the quiet growing outward from where I stood. The groups of disputants and discussers also fell silent and the men began making their way around the yard equipment to the space before my keg.

"I speak here, as you all know, in the name of the Sons of Liberty of this colony, who are striving to preserve our freedoms. The Sons are thrilled and inspired by Boston's fitting reply to the snare-setters and schemers in Parliament; and the time has come, we feel, when New York, too, must decide what it will do about the newly taxed tea which now approaches our shores.

"Our Assembly—supposedly our very own legislature—is a pack of Tories and cravens, utterly under the thumb of the king's governor, and they will not speak or act for us. If we would preserve the liberties that make us men we must act for ourselves. If we would protect our pittances it is we who must oppose the greedy grasp of Parliament. I need not labor these considerations. You understand them well enough. I but remind you of them.

"The Sons of Liberty have called a meeting of the people for noon today to take the sense of the citizenry on these matters. Let no man who values his daily bread or the bread of his children fail to join the parade in which we shall march to the meeting place on the Common!"

I pointed directly before me to where the parade line should begin forming and two adherents of the Sons promptly went to the spot.

Shouts of assent and approval came from the men.

"We're with you, Jamie!"

"Hurrah for Holland tea!"

"New York's harbor is just as good a teakettle as Boston's!"

And with much good-natured jostling they fell into a rough column.

My heart expanded at their ready spirit. These shipyard mechanics—*Hardy's* shipyard mechanics, as Alexander MacDougall and John Lamb called them—were the solidest support of the patriot cause. Perhaps they were not so rapidly stirred to action as the sailors, yet, when aroused, they were more manageable and less given to violence for its own sake—that grinning specter which, once glimpsed, remains forever stark in the mind of any who must incite the multitude.

From outside the shipyard gates at this moment came the rattle and crash of a pair of drums; then another annunciatory ruffle and another; and then, in stimulating cadences, flourish after flourish was beat. A fife picked up the rhythm and began shrilling a marching melody.

I jumped down from my keg and placed myself at the head of the column, and we marched through the gates out into Division Street, greeting the musicians who were waiting there. Without missing a beat they took up a position in front of us and we turned south.

All over the town similar parades were forming, and we could hear their drummers as they, too, set out on their march to the Common.

Over the pressing sense of determination with which we had started, there began to spread a lighter, holiday mood, due perhaps to the music and, perhaps, also to that feeling of well-being men experience when they march of their own will in a body. Banter and chaff began to pass up and down the column, along with much good advice to George the Third.

At Blackwell's rope walk, a block below the shipyard, we could see on the other side of the street fence a column like our own being formed by the rope makers. It seemed to me that a goodly number of them remained, hesitant, at their work and that Caleb Greene, the Son of Liberty in charge here, was having difficulty. I swung our column into Blackwell's lot, drums and fife playing, circled the place, and brought the parade to a halt.

"Come along, men," I called. "This is too important a matter over which to fear Blackwell and his Royal Navy contract. I offer the protecting arm of the Sons of Liberty to any man Blackwell persecutes for leaving his work today. We will be glad to teach Blackwell such a lesson that all the other Tories in this town will read it with ease. Come, have no fear!"

I had struck at the true cause of their hesitancy. They looked at their neighbors and companions of the shipyard, who gazed back at them from our column; and, at first somewhat slowly, but then with spirit of their own, they began sidling out of the aisles in which their work was arranged. I held our column waiting till the very last man had left his task and joined his fellows, and then, signaling the fife and drum to begin again, we marched off out of the rope walk lot.

An air of excitement and expectancy filled the streets. Tradesmen and housewives waited outside shops to watch us go by. Other mechanics, also on their way to the meeting, hastened on the walks alongside us, like outriders, or fell in boldly with our growing parade line. Gentlemen in broadcloth and cocked hats stood stock still, leaning on their walking sticks, and watched us with amazement.

At the foot of lower Division Street began the wide plain of the Common, extending three blocks westward to Broadway and five blocks farther south to Dyes Street. As our procession entered upon the field I saw already gathered there what must have been some fifteen hundred or two thousand people—by far the largest such assemblage I had ever seen. They stood crowded into the northwest corner in a great uneven triangle, facing a rough platform of planks behind which, across the street on private ground purchased by the Sons of Liberty, stood our seventy-foot-high Liberty Pole, proudly flying its pennant.

We of the shipyard closed in across the rear of the large crowd and thereafter we lost our separate identity.

Most of those present were mechanics and journeymen, as could be seen from their thick, black outer coats, their gray or red woolen hats, and their plentifully wound shawls. Around the edges of the dark mass, however, were sprinkled a surprisingly large number of cocked hats and fur-collared broadcloths. Students from King's College mingled with carters and cobblers. Spice importers from South Street elbowed water sellers and joiners. The whole town, apparently, sensed that Boston's tea dumping had brought our difficulties with Britain to a critical pass.

All at once there came a hush over the forward part of the crowd. People at the rear began to strain forward and call "Shush!" John Lamb had mounted the platform, tall, big-boned, and black-haired. With a grave mien and a quiet certainty he waited for the hubbub to subside.

"My fellow citizens of New York," he began, his voice, with its characteristic rasp, deep and penetrating. "My

31

fellow citizens—unenfranchised, as by far the most of you are, as well as those who enjoy the great right to cast a vote. It is an imposition and even a cruelty to call you out upon this unprotected and windy plain in the middle of winter. But our manner of government leaves us no other way to take the opinion of the people.

"Did we all enjoy the privilege to vote, such demonstrations in the open would not be needed. But of the twenty thousand souls who inhabit this colony not so much as a twentieth part have a voice in its government. And yet, it is this unenfranchised bulk of the citizenry who must now provide the strength with which to protect what liberties we have. For the tiny fraction who churlishly monopolize the powers of government have not in themselves the strength to do so.

"Such being the case, we trust you will bear with the inconveniences of this mode of action for the sake of what is as precious to us as our very lives—preserving those liberties and freedoms we already enjoy.

"The king's ministry and Parliament, more clever by far than they need be were they men of honor and of good intent, having concentrated their newest schemes for enslaving us upon the single item of tea, have just received a reply. Boston town, first to receive a consignment of taxed tea, has taken this tea—which the royal pharaoh set over them was insistent upon forcing into their homes—and has pitched it into the sea."

A roar as of a wind rising in a wood came out of the multitude. "Hooray"s and "God bless Boston"s were lost in a general, vast reverberation of approval. The drums began pounding.

Lamb raised his hand and after a while the tumult receded.

"The Sons of Liberty have also received news from sea captains just arrived that tea-bearing ships destined for our own town of New York are close enough to make port at any hour."

Groans, shouts, and imprecations filled the air.

"Burn the ships!"

"Yes, like the Gaspee!"

"Let's go Boston one better!"

"Swing the captains from their yards!"

Lamb again held up his hand.

"This meeting has been called to place before you for your consideration two matters. First, the fact of Boston's courageous and unequivocating action."

Applause, shouts, and drum beatings broke out again.

"And second, the question: What shall we of New York do about the tea that is now nearing our own shores? Shall we quietly pay the tax and accept the act of Parliament as final?"

"No, no, no!" came from hundreds of throats.

"Shall we pay the tax on the tea and give King George the money with which to pay his henchmen—his governors and his judges and his noble generals—so that they can be made utterly independent of our assemblies and the more easily set England's foot on our neck? Shall we help bind the slave's collar around our neck?"

"*No, no!*" came again, this time in even greater volume.

"Or shall we, perhaps, pursue a course which some among us call the only lawful and orderly one? Let the tea be landed, say these counselors, and let it be stored in our

33

warehouses. Once stored, say they, we can then urge our shopkeepers not to accept it for sale; and we can urge our citizens not to buy it at the shops."

The audience waited, uneasy at this seemingly feasible plan, one against which they could think of no objection, yet against which their instincts warned.

Lamb, the experienced orator, paused to let the tension mount.

"I say to such counselors that were we all of us the patriots we ought to be, there would be nothing to fear in such a course. But, alas, there are merchants among us who would soon enough discover the back doors to these warehouses, and there are shopkeepers among us who would quietly sell this cheaper tea—yes, cheaper in spite of the tax—disguised in wrappings of various sorts. And, most lamentable of all, there are among us those who would not be able to resist buying it and drinking it for its cheapness of the moment.

"This, indeed, is what is so clever in London's scheme. They have so sharply reduced the price of tea for their own purpose at this time that even after we pay the tax it will still be cheaper than our own smuggled teas. They expect and know that many among us will not be able to restrain ourselves from buying it. And thus they mean to habituate us to paying the tax. And, with our own resources, we shall be undone as a free people!"

"NEVER, NO, NEVER!" came the roaring response from the crowd.

"How, then, how shall we forestall all this?" Here Lamb paused dramatically. "In one way, and in one way only: The tea must not be allowed to so much as land upon these shores. It must not touch our wharves. It must not be taken off its ships. Do you agree?"

"YES, YES!" Again the drums began to pound.

Lamb held up both hands, as though while trying to still the crowd he at the same time blessed them.

"The Sons of Liberty have prepared a number of resolutions which we now shall present for your consideration. We greatly hope that they will meet with your approval; that you will find them expressive of your true opinions."

Someone standing close to the front of the platform handed up to him a sheet of paper and from this he read aloud: "Resolved, that whoever shall aid or abet or in any manner assist in the introduction of tea from any place whatsoever into this colony, while it is subject by an act of Parliament to the payment of a duty for the object of raising a revenue in America, he shall be deemed an enemy to the liberties of America."

He looked at the gathering and demanded, "Do you so resolve?"

"AYE," came a tremendous shout. Again the drums beat and the fifes shrilled. This time he had to hold both hands aloft for a long time before he could go on.

He read out again from the paper: "Resolved, that whoever shall be aiding or assisting in the landing or carting of such tea from any ship or vessel, or shall hire any house, storehouse, or cellar, or any place whatsoever to deposit the tea, subject to a duty as aforesaid, he shall be deemed an enemy to the liberties of America."

He looked up again and again demanded, "Are you so resolved?"

35

"AYE," came the great, booming reply, filling the air of the Common from boundary to boundary.

"Resolved, that whosoever shall sell or buy or in any manner contribute to the sale or purchase of tea, subject to duty as aforesaid, or shall aid or abet in transporting such tea by land or water from this city, until the Revenue Act shall be totally and clearly repealed, he shall be deemed an enemy to the liberties of America.

"Do you so resolve?"

"AYE," came the now familiar roar.

"Now, then," he went on, "this town must make ready to put its intentions into effect. A watch must be organized forthwith to patrol our wharves. When tea-bearing ships arrive we must be prepared to deal with them. The Sons of Liberty have already begun to make plans toward this end and all able-bodied men who wish to participate in such a watch are asked to present themselves to Jamie Hardy at Hampden Hall. Should you fail to find him in at the Hall you may look for him at the Spread Sail Inn. Or you may leave your name for him at either place."

Lamb drew himself up. "As we are most of us shopkeepers and mechanics who may not spare more of our time from our occupations I shall now call this meeting to an end. The Sons of Liberty will hold themselves ready, henceforth, to convene you again whenever events shall make it desirable. God bless us all!"

The drums pounded and the fifes screamed and the great crowd cheered and shouted as Lamb waved to them. Then he left the platform, and the closely packed throng loosened and began to disperse.

4.

I HAD BEEN at work in the shipyard scarcely fifteen minutes when a messenger arrived to say that the Committee of Inspection was holding an emergency meeting at the Kluger house and urgently desired my presence there.

I excused myself to Eben Stone, who was in charge of the yard and who was an adherent of the Sons of Liberty, and left.

The streets were yet filled with evidences of the public meeting. Crowds lingered at the heads of the avenues that led away from the Common, and smaller groups stood about on the sidewalks outside the taverns and at the street crossings.

As I came down upon the Bowling Green district I saw that even this most sedate enclave was showing signs of agitation. Drawn up about the Kluger gateway and filling the thoroughfare around the circular park were many carriages, quite as though a ball were going on within. The horses trampled and whinnied against the cold, the coach-men slapped themselves across the arms and marched about to keep warm, and all in all the scene bespoke a gathering too hastily called for proper arrangements to have been made on behalf of the servants and horses.

At the white doors of the mansion my knock was answered by a manservant who took my coat and shawl, and, apparently under orders to hurry, guided me quickly through the hallway till we came to that same drawing room in which I had been a guest the evening before.

One glance from the threshold told me the tale. Here was no meeting in progress, but rather the setting for a confrontation. Additional chairs had been introduced, and fifteen or twenty committee members sat waiting. Most were bewigged and powdered, and all wore the broad-cloths, silk stockings, and silver shoe buckles of our prosperous merchants. The majority pulled spitefully on long pipes or moodily sipped flip. Those who did not appear sullen or impatient seemed downright angry.

I little doubted it was myself for whom they waited, even before the first one to sight me let out a sharp "Aha!"

Martin Kluger came forward quickly. "Welcome, Mr. Hardy," he said. "We have been holding up the meeting until your arrival."

The characteristic twinkle occupied his eyes but there was also anxiety in his face. Then I saw standing at one side of the room, in a light blue gown, the slender figure of Elisabeth Kluger. She was apparently acting as her father's hostess.

Some rudiments of the statesmanlike qualities I admired in others stirred within me at sight of her, and I determined to restrain my penchant for flinging down gauntlets.

I said, "Gentlemen, it is as usual a pleasure to meet with you. Shall we proceed?"

Snorts of outrage came from several. "Shall we proceed,

indeed!" shouted old Dinwiddie. "Perhaps the question rather is: Shall we cease proceeding? Shall we cease exciting the rabble and pushing them in the direction of Boston? Shall we cease pushing the heads of our associates into the hangman's noose for treason?"

Above the bluish sacs that hung upon his heavy, mottled face his eyes rolled, marvelously widened and wild.

Kluger interposed. "Counselor Dinwiddie means we have called this meeting because many of us are disturbed by the events on the Common this noon. We feel no time should be lost before discussing it with the Sons of Liberty."

"I will be happy to explain the attitudes of the Sons and to carry back to them whatever of your opinions you charge me to," I replied. "I shall also bear in mind, as I hope you gentlemen will, too, that our dispute is with England and not with one another. By 'rabble' I suppose Counselor Dinwiddie means the bulk of our citizenry. I would point out to him that I, too, am of just such as he describes so uncharitably. Yet he has come here today to meet with me and has even been pleased to wait upon my arrival."

Dinwiddie rose to his feet purple and choking. "Pleased to wait upon your arrival!" he gasped out. "From the very start I said that to entertain among us the opinions of the Sons would lead to ruin. And so it is turning out. For myself, I quit this course of treason and this most perilous encouragement of the riffraff here and now!"

He shoved his chair away and excitedly pushed through the crowded room till he stood near the doorway, where he turned. "Mark me, now, the rest of you. These Sons of Liberty will soon be leading you all by the nose. And when they succeed in giving every lout and every tenant of debtor's prison a vote, they will raise a host against you which will do nothing less than tear your property out of your hands. This is their real aim. The king and a strong government have protected property against the envy of the mob till now. True, we are having our differences with the king. But to call upon the rabble for aid is folly to madness. You are unleashing such forces which will send us all to perdition. This and nothing else is the end to which your actions are leading!"

With that, jowls aquiver, he flung out of the meeting.

I felt quietly elated. Some opinions I differed with. Some angered me. But the self-righteous arrogance of Dinwiddie's kind of privileged wealth aroused in me nothing less than hatred. I was more than satisfied to have him clearly on the other side and to have narrowed to this extent the range of views that prevailed among the patriots.

I turned to the others. "With respect to the meeting on the Common, gentlemen," I said, "I would bring to your attention that most of the people of this colony have no other way to express their opinion. I would remind you that time and again we have asked your support in our attempts to broaden the franchise, but that always, for one reason or another, you refuse to league with us to alter the charter. How else would you have us unite and rally the citizenry, such being the case?"

"Never mind the accursed franchise," called out Daniel Robbins, a thin-visaged silk importer from South Street. "You are forever finding opportunity to introduce it. What rouses our concern right now is that without consulting us the Sons of Liberty are spurring the people to act upon a program the Sons have devised solely themselves. They are being roused and sworn to prevent any landing of tea while lawful methods of action are being deliberately excluded from their consideration. Lawful methods exist and the people can be just as well influenced to try them. That is what we take exception to, and most strenuously. We wish the Sons to desist from this course!"

Shouts of agreement from others endorsed the angry speech.

"I must take exception to your separation of the franchise question from the tea problem," I replied. "Since you help deny us the vote you also free the hands of the Sons to appeal to the citizenry in such terms as we choose. Were you to aid the people at large to achieve a voice in the government you would create a situation in which you, too, could present your views before them and argue to gain acceptance of these views. But this you will not do. As you persist in going your own way, perhaps the Sons have the right to do likewise."

"Blackmail!" someone shouted.

"Progress," I retorted.

"Come, come, we are foundering again upon the same old rock of the franchise. The new circumstances confronting us are too fraught with peril for that. There must be a meeting of attitudes between us and the Sons."

It was Kluger who spoke, reasoningly and chidingly. And with a show of genuine concern and impartiality he spoke as much to the others as to me.

"Suppose, then, gentlemen," I said, "suppose I ask the Sons not to proceed against the tea with violence before gaining the assent of this committee. What will you offer in return? Will you support us in altering the charter of this colony so the greater number of the citizenry may be enfranchised?"

Silence smothered the room. I looked from one face to

another. Above the ruffles and laces and under the powdered wigs the features were set in sullenness or creased in perplexity. The eyes of many glared back in anger for thus being placed at bay.

I said, "It is the old game, then, of getting the chestnuts out of the fire, is it not, gentlemen? You wish to avail yourselves of the numbers and strength of the commonalty in your tax and trade dispute with the lords and merchants of England, but you do not wish to give us a share in the government. Well, then, gentlemen, you must not be overly surprised if we go our own way and enfranchise ourselves.

"You will excuse me now. Last night the Sons set up a watch along the wharves to guard against the arrival of tea and I have been charged with maintaining the watch. I must be off to see that all is in order."

I turned to Kluger, who was now standing beside me. "I regret this impasse, sir. Perhaps the committee of the Sons will be willing to compromise the issue somewhat. I cannot, by myself, say."

"We ought all to regret it, Hardy," he answered, his brow furrowing. "I fear that neither these gentry nor the Sons may understand the gravity of the approaching crisis sufficiently. Unity of effort amongst us has become far and above all else the most important consideration, yet we are failing to achieve it."

He put his arm around my shoulders, which in that outraged assemblage was an act of no mean political significance, and thus, still talking to me, accompanied me out of the room.

"I had asked that this meeting be held in my own house in the hope that I might act somewhat as a mediator, but I'm afraid it has been to no avail."

42

Just then Elisabeth Kluger came out of the meeting room, her dark eyes and quick-moving figure expressing the excitement roused by what she had seen.

"Ah, then," she exclaimed, "you really and truly are leaving the meeting, Mr. Hardy. And now what will become of the American cause, with its forces divided?"

"Shall I tell you, Miss Kluger?"

"Yes, yes, please do!"

"Why, we shall win through against the English on every count that is important to us, although exactly how remains as yet unclear to me."

"Bravo!" she cried, clapping her hands.

It was merest accident that I had visited the Kluger home the previous evening, and it was accident again that I was here today. Two such accidents together were rare indeed and a third might well be beyond recurrence. All at once it seemed to me it would be a most foolish denial of fateful opportunity for me merely to smile politely at her and take my leave courteously, thereafter only to hope that our paths might cross again.

"Miss Kluger," I said, "would you like to accompany me on my round of visits to the wharves this afternoon? I think you will gain a view of our city which you might not otherwise, and find it of interest to see at first hand how we manage our affairs. While the day is cold the weather is tolerable enough for a walk. And it won't take you from your household duties for more than an hour—at the most, perhaps an hour and a half."

I might have gone on tacking good reason after good reason till the tea ships themselves arrived, had she not glanced beyond me at Kluger.

I could almost feel his nod as her expression changed from amused surprise to assent.

"It sounds delightful. I do think Louisa will be able now to manage with our guests, Father. It will take me only a minute to get a cloak, Mr. Hardy."

And she was away.

Left alone with Kluger, I said, "I hope you don't think me too forward, sir. It did occur to me Miss Kluger might get a somewhat different view of the city."

"I've been a young man myself, Hardy," he replied. "But mind you don't convert her to your wild leveling principles."

"As to that, sir, I would be an unbearably great hypocrite if I promised."

Miss Kluger reappeared wearing a long, light blue cloak, the hood thrown back across her shoulders. Except for silver lace along the sleeves it was extremely plain in design and set off her dark hair and eyes and slender figure with disturbing impact. With a small white muff, the ensemble, in its artful simplicity, struck strongly at its target, if the effect on the opposite sex was the aim. Even Kluger paused thoughtfully, as though he was suddenly seeing his daughter in a new light.

"Good day, sir," I said to him. "I shan't keep the young lady out long."

5.

ON THE SIDEWALK we paused to choose our direction. Her presence induced an unexpected exhilaration in me—strong enough to supplant much of the angry excitement of the meeting we had just left.

As I glanced about I saw the familiar scene afresh for the moment, somewhat as she, one long absent, might be viewing it.

We were almost as far south on the island as it was possible to be, and between the bare trees and the widely spaced houses we could see gleaming quite close the silver of both rivers as they converged toward the bay. On our left hand, west of Broadway, handsome gardens were laid out, which, within half a mile northward, grew into fine farms neatly set among the woodlands. To our right, along the East River bank, sat the town proper; and from this direction the yellows and crimsons and blues of the Dutch-style bricks peeped out from among the trees with sober and quiet charm.

We were but a small town, after all, as cities were reckoned in Europe—possibly a mile in length and not over half a mile in width—and presented no spectacular engineering works as perhaps a city should. We boasted no stone-worked palaces nor great buildings of government nor the marvelous congestions of population about which I had read and heard. Our numbers totaled possibly seventeen thousand. Few of our houses were more than two stories high, and most of them were of wood; only those of the well-to-do were of colored Dutch tiles or brick. For the rest, our architecture was summed up in the modest steeples of Saint Paul's and Trinity and in the City Hall, somewhat north and eastward of us.

"There is an odd look in your eyes, Mr. Hardy," Elisabeth Kluger said smilingly, as she saw my gaze linger on the roof of the City Hall.

"There are five hundred muskets stored in that building," I said to her.

"Mr. Hardy," she exclaimed, "I do believe poor old Mr. Dinwiddie may be right, after all, when he says you propose treason."

I laughed. "But you will not turn me over for treason, as Dinwiddie would?"

"Why, no—not as yet, I suppose."

She was still smiling, but at the same time looked carefully into my face to see whether I was joking. It occurred to me that the way she wore her black hair, parted in the center and drawn back close to her head, was most effective.

As though reminded by my glance she pulled on her hood, tied the strings under her chin, and then buried her hands in her muff, all with gestures that were graceful and feminine yet straightforward.

When she was ready we made our way around the little

park; and as we entered the side streets I wished that it were spring and that the oaks and maples along the walks were in foliage. It would have reminded her how pretty a town New York could be, quite like a collection of houses set down in a garden. Old London could never have presented an appearance so fresh and colorful.

"How long did you stay in England?" I asked.

"A little over two years."

"A long visit!"

"Perhaps. I myself began to think so. The fine houses in town and country, the servants everywhere, the parties and visitings and masques, all of which I was so taken with at first—it turned out there was nothing more. Certainly not for women."

She walked on in silence and I watched her intently, trying to gauge this hint of depths.

"Yet, surely," I said, with a slight flurry of newly discovered anxiety, "there must have been young men there who took an interest in so— In such a— Whose interest would enliven—"

"Oh, there were. Fops and dandies. Their greatest attainments were judging horses and dogs and making irresponsible approaches to the ladies."

She turned to me, a slight frown of determination on her oval, dark-eyed face. "Perhaps I'm my father's daughter. Father took a small inheritance and created out of it a fleet of merchant ships and an important position in this colony. His life's blood is to do and to build. I believe I judge circumstances and men according to what I've observed of him. And at times I wish I'd been born a man so I could be free to work and to build, too, and go about freely and speak my mind straightforwardly."

Her delicate nostrils flared with protest. "When Father told me to return home till the differences with England were patched up, I looked forward to it with interest. But I find here much the same wearying emptiness. Especially among the women. I've been to the assemblies and the routs of the Beekmans and the De Lanceys and the Livingstons, and they have been to our house, and we have gone the rounds that way twice now this season, and perhaps we will go them again. It all seems much the same as in England, only a ridiculously crude imitation."

She walked on, looking directly before her, brows no longer serene.

I said, "It may well be that your difficult fate is to be your father's daughter."

"Why 'difficult fate'?"

"Because I think you truly have an instinct for doing, but in our day women are ordained to do nothing. They are to breed children within marriage so that accumulated property is correctly handed on. And for the rest they are to chatter about fashions. And when, soon enough, their husbands find them dull, and take to entertaining themselves outside the home, they are trained not to notice."

"Ah, you are preaching, just as you did at dinner in our house, and to the Committee. I begin to recognize the tone! Tell me, then, is there room among those ideas of yours for women who feel they want to live otherwise?"

"Of course there is! It is part of the democratic view, which is for all people. We want the very same chance at a meaningful life for women as we want for men. We don't know the modes for achieving it yet. Perhaps our political forms will have to alter, first. But such is without question one of our aims."

She stared at me now, both of us heedless of the walkway ahead, her deep black eyes rapt, as though something significant within her had been stirred. I sensed that for the moment she was almost disoriented with new considerations.

I do not know by what miracle of obedience to the rules of deportment I did not take her in my arms, then and there, upon the street, and tell her I would do anything on earth one human being could do for another. But I did not. Instead, I shook my head slowly in confirmation.

And my reward was a slow-dawning, frank, almost intimate smile.

We entered the wharfside streets and the character of the scene began to change. Pleasant dwellings set back upon their lawns gave way now to warehouses and counting houses whose doors opened directly on the sidewalks. The windowless, blind sides of the warehouses were built right up against the street line and as we neared the river they increased in size and came closer together, crowding out sky and trees.

An odor charged the atmosphere, strange and pungent, almost offensively sharp, yet exciting to the senses. In it mingled the exhalations of the exotic spices stored in the warehouses, the smells of leather and pitch and salt-encrusted sails and timbers, and the damp odor of the river itself, borne in by the brisk breeze.

"The odors of the wharves don't bother me," I said, grateful for a different topic of conversation. "Rather, sometimes, they make me impatient with laboring day after day in the shipyard, and I want to go off as a sailor to see the distant places of the world."

She smiled her frank smile again, her eyes less sad. "Ah, then there is more to you than the politician!"

The warehouses now abruptly ceased altogether, and we found ourselves looking out across Dock Street, broad and cobble-paved and teeming with people and horses and carts. On the other side flowed the river.

Here Murray's Wharf sent its staunch underpinnings far out into the swirling waters. Today, two vast-bellied ocean sailing ships were moored against it, their sails furled, their hatch covers off, and their incoming and outgoing cargoes piled in heaps and mounds the length of the wharf and out onto the street for a block and more in either direction. Sailors, draymen, and merchants swarmed around the hillocks of merchandise, buying and selling, judging, haggling and remonstrating, and doing it all swiftly and purposefully.

"Don't you find it exciting?" I asked.

She nodded, her senses quickening at the sight.

I led the way out into the throngs. The cargoes formed lanes and alleys upon the broad thoroughfare, and within these, the contrasts of color and odor were wonderful: Here the foul stench of piled hides, there the sweet, heavy aroma of wine in straw-protected bottles, and a little beyond, overpowering them both, the sharp tang of tobacco in hogsheads. Through it all we had to dodge the quick-working loaders and carters, who seemed to care about nothing but their goods.

A block northward along this busy bazaar stood Gulie's Tavern, the base for the two men who had been chosen as observers for this part of the waterfront. From a distance I could see neither of them, but as we came closer young Jack Woolton appeared from behind a wall of baled furs.

"Here I be, Jamie!" he exclaimed, catching my arm.

"Aaron Fletcher is about, patrolling, too. We've examined every box and bundle on the wharf. There's no tea. Not yet, anyhow."

"Good, Jack. And what are you to do if you find any?"

"One of us is to go to Hampden Hall to tell whoever is in charge."

"And if there is no one at the Hall?"

"We are to find you at the shipyard or at the Spread Sail Inn."

"Leaving a note behind you, meanwhile, at the Hall."

"Yes—leaving a note telling the ship and the wharf and the time of day the note was writ."

"Just so. Good!"

Jack was a round-faced, energetic lad of about seventeen. He was apprenticed to a baker who was one of the Sons and who permitted him to serve on the watch during hours when he might otherwise have been at the ovens. He was thickset and well muscled and I had selected him, like all the others, with one eye on his ability to acquit himself in a scuffle.

As we talked, Aaron Fletcher, the second observer, came up. Aaron was a slow-speaking man about five years my senior, thin of lip and firm of jaw. I had myself interested him in the activities of the Sons. He was a joiner and I had met him first at Malfi's book store.

"There's no tea about yet, Jamie." His eyes went to Miss Kluger and then back to me.

"Do you detect an attitude of one sort or another about our watch, Aaron?"

" 'Tis a mite early to say. We've dressed soberly and we interfere with no one, just as you've told us, so we stir up little reaction as yet. Some of the Tory merchants give us a black look now and then, but the carters will hold up a load without saying a word, so we may examine it the better."

The confident way his long, thin mouth clamped closed at the end of his statement told me even more.

"You know you're supposed to be relieved at four, Aaron. If your relief fails to arrive exactly in time send Jack to tell me at once. I want the watch to operate just as it should from the very start. You understand, this is an opportunity for us to train ourselves for whatever else may require organized effort."

Aaron nodded.

I said goodbye and Elisabeth Kluger and I resumed our journey up the waterfront.

"Why have you told the men not to dress ostentatiously or to interfere with people?" she asked. "I should have thought you would want to threaten everyone with the knowledge that you were on the watch against tea."

"We don't want to antagonize people needlessly. Everyone already knows the Sons are guarding against tea. For the rest, we'll apply any force that may be needed in concentrated form, where it may produce the best results."

Several blocks farther along was the Beekman slip. Here the base for our observers was the Sign of the Golden Galleon, a chandler's shop that stood a few doors inside Water Street. Again, the observers were out and about their business.

"No tea, Jamie!"

It was Cain Desmond, a strapping young apprentice printer, free of manner and witty of tongue, yet capable of sober thought when it was required.

"No, indeed, Jamie, you can take the lad's word for it. We were over everything on the wharf like a couple of terriers."

This came from Wilfred Hoskins, the second observer here, a mechanic from my own shipyard. Wilfred was older than most of us and married, with two babes. Like some of the others he was already a veteran of a number of fights with the soldiery.

I asked a few questions to satisfy myself that they understood their instructions, cautioned young Desmond not to press too strongly, and told Hoskins to send word to me immediately should his relief fail to arrive in time. Then we continued up the street.

The next team of observers were two of our seamen whose ship was being refitted. With their brightly colored silk head kerchiefs, deeply tanned complexions, and free and easy manners, they appeared out of place, exotic. There was no tea found on their wharf either. I reminded them of the details of their instructions and we moved on.

At last we stood at the northern end of Cherry Street, where the river bends westward a little to form a small shoulder on the land, and the wharves end.

Our watch organization was a great success, it seemed to me. We were mustering a spirited group of energetic and intelligent young men whose confidence and willingness were of the highest. Not only would no tea land in New York; more important for what we had in mind, we had a group of men who could stand up to whatever perils the dispute might bring.

After a short pause we began the return journey. The trip along the wharves had taken us almost an hour, but despite my best efforts to prolong it, the way back, down Broadway, took us little more than twenty minutes.

When we were almost at the gates of her house Elisabeth Kluger said, "I wish to express my resentment that every

53

journeyman on the wharves may address you as Jamie but that I must remain on such distant terms as to call you Mr. Hardy. May I not call you Jamie, too?"

"Of course!"

"Thank you. You may call me Elisabeth if you wish."

"I do wish."

I hardly noticed that we had arrived at the wrought iron gates.

"Elisabeth, may I call for you again?"

"You may."

"We seem to meet always in the midst of crowds—committee meetings and tea watches—"

"But we first met with only my father present." Her eyebrows rose in mock surprise at my forgetting.

"The worst crowd of all! I should like to have somewhat less of the world's hubbub about us. Do you think it possible?"

"Perhaps."

She put out her white-gloved little hand. "Good afternoon, Jamie Hardy. Thank you for a most interesting walk."

6.

IN THE COOL, EARLY MORNING, the Kluger carriage came up the road, its slender, brightly lacquered wheels and the footfalls of the horses impressing almost soundlessly into the soft, much-traveled earth of upper Broadway. Elisabeth opened the door and I got in.

We sat and looked at each other in greeting, both of us trying to smile a little, trying to recapture something of the intimacy of our trip along the wharves the other day, yet feeling more truly on edge, and even apprehensive.

"Tell him to take the highway to Greenwich," I said. "The views across the river there are striking."

Elisabeth called her instructions up to the coachman and then lifted the lid of a straw hamper that stood on the floor.

"You see, we have all sorts of good things to eat—sliced duck and chicken, and jams. And jugs of coffee. For I knew you wouldn't drink tea. We'll have a glorious picnic. You don't think the ground will be too damp to sit on? I've brought blankets."

"A good precaution."

"Do you know, I haven't gone on a picnic since I was a little girl—since long before I left for England."

"Don't the English go on picnics?"

She laughed. "Oh, no. They go away to the country—to huge mansions and castles in landscaped parks. One wears even finer clothes in the country than in London."

We were driving close beside the Hudson now. The broad sheet of sparkling water reflected the white clouds and the light blue sky. Through the dark trees we could see patches of new grass. On the other side of the river stood the Palisades, rising straight up from the water's edge like great-shouldered, dignified sentinels guarding the way to the continent beyond.

I watched loose wisps of her hair rise and fall with the breeze that came through the windows, and her fine profile, illuminated by the sunlight.

She turned from the window and smiled, perhaps as a bit of an apology for having lost herself in her thoughts.

"I'm so glad you invited me to go along with you when you inspected the tea watch. I've been thinking of it ever since. It was most exciting."

"The real excitement will come if the British insist on landing tea," I replied.

For some reason my words came stiffly and I felt awkward. I didn't want to discuss politics.

"Perhaps I should say it's you I've been thinking about," she said. "All those men on the tea watch hung upon your every word and gesture. I suppose you realized that?"

"Well, I'm in charge of the tea watch and so they're attentive to what I say."

She laughed, a soft, musical double note. "It's a great deal more than that. Father would say you're a natural-born leader. And you speak very well. Yet, you can't have attended King's College. I intend no offense, of course. I'm judging by your occupation."

"In these colonies a shipwright who has a taste for learning is free to take all sorts of roads to knowledge."

"You haven't been to school at all, then?"

"I've had as much instruction as a master is bound to allow an apprentice, which is to say some schooling at spelling and ciphering and then the practices of my trade. For the rest, my schools have been the debating club and the book store."

"The debating club?"

"Till recently some of us gathered together one evening a week to discuss literature and events. We would decide beforehand on something to read, say Rousseau's *Social Contract*, or Montesquieu's *Spirit of Laws*, and then, at the meeting, we would debate its meanings and merits. We've had to give it up, though. There's no time for it these days."

"How remarkable!" she exclaimed.

"Remarkable?"

"That you should be so bent on learning and understanding."

I had in times past thought about this myself and had arrived at an explanation. But an inner voice warned me against setting it forth here and now. I would have to divulge things about myself that would be better left to a more propitious moment.

"Perhaps," I replied. "Come, let's look about. Can anything be prettier than what we have here? I think this is where we ought to halt."

We were overlooking a broad stretch of grassy bank sloped to the water's edge, affording a view of the river for great distances in either direction.

"Yes, it's very pretty," she agreed. "Benjamin," she called up to the coachman, "stop here. And come help us carry the things out."

"Tell him to look to the horses," I said. "I'll take care of the basket and the blankets."

We went out on the grass, leaving Benjamin behind with the carriage, and spread two blankets close to the crest of the decline.

Elisabeth drew a deep breath. "It's inspiring here."

"Yes," I replied, pointing across the river to the high walls of the Palisades. "Those cliffs always remind me of the continent waiting beyond, a huge land that dwarfs Europe the way this blanket dwarfs a handkerchief. No white man has really seen it yet, but we know it's vast and fertile. The Mississippi measures its width at its mouth in miles, and its waters are heavy with the earth it carries."

"You sound almost reverent," Elisabeth said softly. "Why should you care so much about an uninhabited stretch of land, no matter how big it is?"

"Because it's a new chance given by God to humanity. Unshackled by the social, feudal depravities of Europe, a better world might be created on it. There is enough land so everyone may farm for himself, without being a serf or tenant. Each might own for himself and raise families with all the virtues that spring from independence and self-reliance. That's the promise of the empty continent beyond those hills."

She studied me. Then she said wonderingly, "Jamie, how is it you concern yourself with such things?"

"I can't sit by and watch this marvelous dream destroyed by the traditions and laws of the greedy, pretentious little knot of people who have trained us to consider them our lords and betters. I couldn't bear to see these countless millions of acres casually given over in vast tracts to the Earl This and the Marquis That so they might later parcel them out to serfs and tenants and carry on the wretched European mode here."

She put her hand on mine. "Mind, I am not disputing, but I, for one, have never even dreamt of these things. How is it everyone does not see matters this way?"

"Most of us are taught from birth to believe that things are as they are because they are rightly so. That's what binds down the landless and the poor. The rich and noble, of course, have no reason to see things otherwise." I hesitated, and then added, "And few among the poor have a special stimulus to see things differently, such as, say, having had a father who was hanged at Newgate."

"And was your father hanged at Newgate?"

"Yes."

I was aware that her hand tightened on mine, and did not move away.

"Why? What for? What had he done?"

"He had committed the crime of being born a yeoman in the county of Suffolk in England."

"I don't understand, Jamie. Tell me why."

"The lords of England have been busy enacting statutes enclosing the common lands. Which is to say, sitting as Parliament, they are voting to themselves the great areas which have been tilled freely by the yeomanry of England since medieval times. And the Lords have also discovered that raising sheep for wool is more profitable and less troublesome than dealing with farmers. They've forced hundreds of thousands of yeomen off the land and into the cities, where there's no work to be had. My father was one of these.

"I have been told that he wasn't the sort of man to seek oblivion in gin, as so many others in this same miserable plight did, but when it came to starvation he brought himself to steal. My mother was pregnant and ill, and one day, in his desperation, he seized some rolls in a bakeshop. Unfortunately he was rather inept as a thief, and they caught him on the spot. The penalty in England for stealing food is death by hanging."

She sat beside me in silence, a silence that would have fired my indignation were it not for the tight hold she kept of my hand.

I could not stop myself from adding, "So you see, that noble manner of living is truly expensive. Those silks and servants and country houses cost the lives of many, many of England's yeomanry."

When at last she spoke, reflectively and very slowly, she said, "There are great areas in London, frightful areas, given over entirely to the wretched. We never drove through them except by accident or when in a great hurry, and my companions viewed their denizens as a dangerous congeries of near-animals." She paused. "Must such things really be, Jamie? I can scarcely tell you how overwhelmed I was each time chance made me aware of these people."

"Overwhelmed with fear, do you mean? There'd be much to fear, true enough."

"No, with horror. And with great pity. At how starved, how misshapen, how less than human these people were. And when I would ask, 'Couldn't something be done?' I was always told no. I was assured this is what ordinary folk are like and this is the difference between them and the noble and wealthy. And yet I came from a land that showed almost none of this."

"Even though so many of our settlers were from Europe's lower classes," I added. "Came, many of them, in fact, as indentured servants and as transported criminals. No, it needn't at all be so. But it will be easier to keep this state of affairs from gaining a footing here than later to try to change it."

Still holding my hand tightly, she said, "So you were born in England?"

"No. My mother indentured herself to pay for her passage to this country and I was born after she arrived. But the poor woman died soon after I was born, before she had worked out her indenture. I myself am the foster child, so to speak, of a waterfront hostelry, the Spread Sail Inn."

"That's the inn where you still live?"

"Yes. The good people there had no children of their own at the time, and the woman had befriended my mother. And even though I was the potboy and worked about the stable and waited upon customers for my keep, they were both fond of me—and are to this very day. When I came of the proper age they apprenticed me to a shipwright and it's something of a true home I've had with them."

"Oh, Jamie! How wonderful! Oh, what a wonderful tale! That from such difficulties you should have made of yourself the person you are!"

Something within me loosened and opened, and as though moved by something outside myself, I drew her gently toward me. Her lips parted ever so slightly as I pressed my own upon them.

For a long moment we sat that way, transported by something utterly unexpected and new-found. Then she put her hand gently against my chest. When we moved apart the world seemed to have altered. Even the quality of the sunshine seemed to have changed.

I examined her lovely oval face as though I were seeing it for the first time. And she, head tilted slightly to one side, her dark eyes deep and serious, appeared to be doing the same with mine.

"I didn't quite intend—" she began in a whisper, haltingly, and then, true to her inner self and unable to play at attitudes, she stopped.

She meant she had surprised herself.

Words would not come for me, either. Nor were they wanted. Her intent, even anxious expression softened to a smile. I drew her to me again and this time her arms went slowly up around my neck and, less surprised, more aware, we tasted of the ecstasy to be found in love.

We were almost different people when we separated. Talking in low tones, uttering only half a phrase at a time, we took picnic things out of the hamper and arranged them on the blanket, our minds still on each other and wondering at the profound feelings that possessed us.

The food before us, we discovered we had no desire to eat. Instead, we rose, and, fingers intertwined, walked down the bank toward the river, stealing glances at each other and corroborating in little ways the marvelous yet fragile new thing between us.

To our astonishment the sun was past the meridian and beginning to make long shadows when we returned to the picnic spread. We gathered up the blankets and cushions and food and carried them out to the road and the waiting carriage.

Stretched in a blanket outside the conveyance, sleeping, lay the coachman. I shook him gently awake and we prepared to go back.

Within the carriage Elisabeth put her arm in mine and we rode in a close, wondering silence.

When the first houses appeared we kissed for the last time and then she called up to the driver. He stopped and I climbed down and waited till the vehicle got into motion again. Then I walked after it in the dusk toward the center of town.

The back yard of the Spread Sail Inn came right down to the East River. A seat was there that had been a favorite place of mine ever since my boyhood, a great wooden beam set along the river's edge at the end of the yard, which served the purpose of a stringpiece. I had spent many hours sitting on it, musing while I listened to the powerful slapping of the water against the piles beneath. I made my way to it now.

I watched the newly appearing stars and it seemed to me that the vast distances across which they signaled corresponded to the feelings that welled up inside me.

At last all the lights had been extinguished along the shore and in the town behind me, and the cold of the night began eating into my bones. With a sense that for once I had no quarrel with my fate I rose and climbed the outside stairway at the rear of the inn to my room.

7.

TEA.

The single word, scrawled in John Lamb's hand on a ragged piece of brown paper, brought me upright on my cot. "Thanks, Tommy."

I dropped the pamphlet I was reading, threw on my street clothing, and raced down the back stairs and across town.

On the upper floor of Hampden Hall a pair of windows was alight, sending their glow out into the treetops like emanations from a brain ceaselessly on guard for the patriot cause. Entering the building I paused only to be recognized by two young fellows who were on watch inside the door.

The old staircase creaked and swayed as I mounted. Unlike the polished, carpeted steps at Montagnie's Inn, these were splintering and bare. And, upstairs, the flooring of the hallway sagged badly away from the stairwell and the walls needed mending. But these were the best quarters the Sons could afford, and for the sake of the hopes to which they gave shelter I had grown fond of them.

The meeting room itself was long and uncomfortably

narrow, and devoid of grace or charm. The unevenly patched walls were graying and gathering dust along the tops of ridges where they bulged and buckled. The worn flooring was uncovered and the dust-caked windows undraped.

Above the fireplace, located unhappily in one of the end walls, was a large, framed picture showing John Hampden in the act of defying King Charles's officers as they demanded ship money. Next to it, pasted directly to the wall with no consideration of proper spacing, was a copy of Revere's engraving of the massacre at Boston in '70. Scattered forlornly on the other walls and separated by great distances which emphasized the bareness of the chamber were portraits of Jean Jacques Rousseau, John Locke, and General Wolfe—this last placed there, doubtless, by an admiring veteran of the French war.

Most of the Sons committee were already present. I took one of the chairs that stood haphazardly about the room and brought it up to the two small tables which had been placed end to end and around which seven committeemen sat.

Alexander MacDougall, who was acting as chairman, said to me, "The ship *Nancy* is at Sandy Hook with a cargo of tea and she only awaits the night tide to bring her in."

The slight burr in his speech that he had brought with him as a child from the Hebrides was more pronounced tonight. And his large, cold Scottish blue eyes glistened with determination. He was the ablest on the committee and he and Lamb were tacitly accepted by the rest of us as the chief leaders of the Sons. Besides an absolutely dauntless courage, which had already seen him jailed for unyielding defiance of the Tory Assembly, he had a razor-keen mind. In his early forties, he managed his successful merchandising business with ease while devoting himself to the broader interests of humanity.

Isaac Sears hunched his burly frame forward over the table and demanded, "Tell us about the tea watch. Have they been patrolling vigorously? Have they made it plain we will bear with no trifling?"

Sears had won a great reputation for daring while commanding privateers during the French war and had become thereafter a favorite of the waterfront crowd—the sailors and ship tenders. A merchandiser by trade, like MacDougall, he had little of MacDougall's acute intelligence or restraint. Though he was over forty, his hair-trigger temper and penchant for immediate battle had to be watched and curbed like that of a fifteen-year-old.

"The spirit of the men is very high," I replied. "Their examination of the wharves is constant and thorough and I have every confidence that no tea will slip past them into the town."

Sears felt he was being contradicted by my even tone and my implied disapproval of needless aggression, and his eyes began to blaze, but MacDougall cut the matter off with, "Now, then, to the chief business. What shall we do about the *Nancy*?"

"Destroy the tea," said Marinus Willett promptly.

I, too, wanted to dump the tea, but I felt this only emotionally, as a fighter feels he wants to return a blow. Willett would be apt to have more reasoned cause than that and I waited to hear it.

Willett's was counted the coolest and levelest judgment on the Sons committee. A graduate, at last, of King's College, he had worked at many things in his life, from the lowly to the grand, till he had become a successful merchant and amassed much real property. And he had won a reputation for courage and keen thinking under fire as a soldier against the French with Abercrombie and Bradstreet.

"The fact is," he said, "that is the only way to align this colony with Boston. And we had best do it as quickly and emphatically as possible. New York is already notorious among our sister colonies for being the weak link in the patriot chain. And situated as we are, at the center, the defection of New York would mean cutting the colonies in two and crippling patriot hopes. The sad truth is that if the issue were put to a vote in this colony, those few with the right to vote, being overly anxious about their property, would vote our cause down."

I understood. And it seemed to me Willett was suggesting a most ingenious political stratagem. By dumping the tea, our relatively small group of the Sons, leading a populace which had no vote, would be circumventing the Tory-filled Assembly and our own patriot but conservative merchants.

Both Lamb and MacDougall were nodding agreement and it was clear what the committee's decision would be, when there came a noise of footsteps pounding hastily up the stairs. A man burst into the room, shawl and hair flying. I recognized him as Fred Hillyer of the tea watch.

"The ship *London* has just arrived on the tide and she is carrying tea!"

"You mean the *Nancy*," I said.

"No, the *London*. She's a second ship and has come up directly to town. The *Nancy* is still at Sandy Hook."

"How do you know she bears tea?" I demanded.

"The sailors coming off her say so. The captain, whom they dislike, is carrying it for his own account."

We stared at him, gauging the probabilities. In a low voice I said to those around the table, "The man is reliable." Aloud, I asked, "Are they unloading?"

"No, not till tomorrow morning. The Customs House is closed this time of night. But the news is spreading along the waterfront and into town and a crowd has begun to gather on Murray's Wharf."

"The Sons' guard mustn't make a move before we say so. You understand that, Freddie?"

"Of course. But suppose the others get impatient? The townspeople at the wharf, I mean?"

"That's as it may be. I doubt they'll actually do anything, at least not this evening. Go back and be vigilant and let us know at the first sign of a move to unload."

"Now, then," said MacDougall after Fred Hillyer had left, "when and how to dump this new shipment of tea? I think it must be tonight and employing the tea watch. What do you say, Jamie?"

"Tonight, yes, before it begins to leave the ship in one way or another, and while we have fewer of the crew to contend with. I expect the sailors will be going ashore to make wassail. It will take me about two hours to get additional men. It is now half past eight. I should be ready at half past ten."

"How many will you take?" Sears asked.

"Twenty men would be enough, but to make sure I'll take thirty."

MacDougall's face creased thoughtfully. "Perhaps you should take more—say, forty. If we failed at just this stage, no matter what the accidental reason, it would greatly injure the step-by-step development of our policy. Can you gather forty men?"

"I believe so. I have seventy-three on the watch from whom to choose."

Again, now, came the noise of running feet upon the stairs, and a group of our guards burst into the room.

"The town is going wild!" the foremost shouted. "Murray's Wharf is crowded with excited people and they're threatening to board the ship. They're convinced she carries tea!"

MacDougall exclaimed, "Whether they're right or wrong, if an unorganized mob is beaten off by the crew it will be as bad in its effect as if we ourselves had failed. Let's hurry down there! Come along!"

We seized hats and cloaks and all rushed pell-mell in a body down the stairs and across the dark town.

As we rounded the corner leading onto Murray's Wharf we came upon an astonishing sight. Against the darkness of the night sky and the black background of the river there flared torches and lanterns amid a mass of people packed onto the wharf so tightly it was a wonder they were not falling off the sides. All were shouting and cheering, their faces uplifted to the great ship moored alongside. Far above, on its deck, there moved other flares and lights. Figures were clambering up the ship's ladders.

While we stared, cries of triumph began to come from above.

"We've found it!"

"Just as they said!"

A great cheer rose along the wharf, drawing itself out into curses and threats. The crowd surged toward the ladders and up the side in two steady streams. From above came the thud and ring of axes on wood and the sound of chests being ripped open.

A splash sounded under the bows as a sizable object struck the river from the heights. The axes rang steadily now. Splash followed splash. And soon we smelled the pungent-sweet odor of tea soaking in river water.

In the flickering torchlight we of the Sons committee looked at one another, silent amid the cries and jostlings of the excited crowd. Our feelings mirrored themselves on our faces: astonishment at the great readiness of the people to act, chagrin at having underestimated their spirit, elation at finding ourselves so heartily endorsed—at being pulled, as it were, for once, instead of always doing the pulling.

"It is done," MacDougall pronounced. "We are one with Boston, now. Not all the resolutions of the Assembly will undo this night's work."

8.

May 1774

"SHOULDER ARMS!"

In two ragged bunchings of motion the forty-odd weapons before me were hoisted from the ground, across the chests of their owners and then up onto their left shoulders. There they wavered against the sky and at length came to a fitful sort of rest.

"No, no, for God's sake, no! If each of you were executing the movements properly all the barrels would be slanting upward at the same angle. And why are so many of you afflicted with the palsy this morning? Can't you hold steady?"

I gave the command for order arms, and after the butts were all back on the ground I again called, "Shoulder arms!"

Again came the two-motion, poorly coordinated heave. Again the three rows of musket barrels wavered crazily, this time—it seemed to me—like the hairs on the back of a caterpillar.

"No, never!" I shouted.

71

I ordered the arms returned to the ground and prepared to give criticism.

"It's all damned foolishness," said Andrew Wiechers, pulling out his pipe and tobacco pouch.

"That it is, Jamie," Hezekiah Greene agreed. "How will 'Keep your wrist at the guard' and 'Seize the firelock just above the swivel' help us to run the redcoats out?"

I pulled *The Complete Drill Sergeant* from my pocket and slapped it. "Exercises like this instill coordination, a sense of unity, and esprit."

"Foolishness," repeated Wiechers. "If I didn't already have esprit I wouldn't be out here of my own free will learning to be a soldier."

Which was true. It was in fact dawning on me as we trained that in large part, and regardless of the fine explanations in the manuals, exercises like this were designed, really, to instill a grudging obedience in men who were soldiers against their will.

"Well," I said, "they also teach you to move in a body—to march and wheel without falling all over one another, and that's extremely important."

"Yes, that's so," Hezekiah agreed. "But we've had enough of this for today. Let's try something else. We'll go back to 'Shoulder arms' and 'Order arms' next Sunday, Jamie, and we'll truly try harder."

"All right. Then I think we should do the platoon exercises next—especially the firing in ranks."

"Better," came from many. Pipes were knocked out and muskets picked up.

As the men resumed their places in the three squads I saw that we had a visitor. Out on the highway a carriage had halted.

"Front rank make ready!" I called.

The men in the first of the three rows sank each to his right knee, at the same time cocking his musket.

"Present!"

The muskets came up to the firing position.

"Fire!"

A handful of metallic clicks sounded as the triggers were pulled; then the line sprang erect and began to load again.

"Center rank make ready!"

They cocked, remained standing, and each man stepped a short pace to the right.

"Present!"

Up came their muskets in the spaces between the men in the front rank.

"Fire!"

The triggers clicked, the muskets were withdrawn, and they began at once to reload.

"Rear rank make ready!"

They cocked and each man took a long step to the right.

"Present!"

Their muskets rose and aimed through the spaces between the men in the first two ranks.

"Fire!"

Another group of clicks sounded, and they too began to reload.

They were getting the hang of this "firing en bloc" very satisfactorily. There wasn't a man present who hadn't been hunting game in these woods since he was ten years old, and so it wasn't surprising that they were quick to master the niceties of firing through ranks.

"That was fine! Absolutely fine!"

Josh Root cleared his throat noisily. "Last week Mr.

MacDougall explained to us how the British used to get beat in the French war because they fought just like this instead of Indian style, each man behind his tree."

"Of course," I replied. "Bloc firing is not always useful. But it has to be learned for times when it might be. In a pitched battle, for instance, when the enemy is advancing toward us over open ground."

Having had his say, Josh relapsed into a satisfied silence. I, for my part, was learning to let men of various stripes give vent to ideas and attitudes.

"Let's go through it again. Remember, a column of redcoats is marching toward you and they are hemmed in by a wall of boulders on one side and the sheer bank of a river on the other. Now, make every bullet count!"

I gave the commands in somewhat quicker tempo this time and they executed them as skillfully as before.

"Once more and we can move on to signals."

"It's noon, Jamie."

"Oh. Too bad. All right, then."

And I dismissed them.

I lingered, finding little things to do till the others had all started off back to town. Through my delays the carriage remained standing on the highway. Now, trailing my musket, I made my way over the grass to it.

The window opened and Elisabeth looked out at me.

Whether love brings the same things to all men I do not know, of course. But I can say that I pity those who have never experienced it. To love and be loved in return must be nothing less than a foretaste of true salvation.

Even when Elisabeth and I differed, as we often did in our political views, our arguments were a challenge and a delight to me.

"Granted that it may not be right for one man to engross hundreds of thousands of acres while so many others starve, landless, as in England," she would say, tentatively and carefully, an utter newcomer to polemics, yet even in her hesitations displaying a mind firm and clear. "Still, the question of suffrage for everyone, as you raise it—isn't that something quite different? And quite dangerous? Is it needful to link the two?"

"But of course!" I would reply, on the instant and all too decisively. And then, remembering myself, more softly, "But how do you mean? Tell me more, first, of why you ask."

"Why, there is the matter of sheer covetousness. There are far more landless and poor than wealthy. If each poor man's vote were equal to a rich man's, the poor would at once vote away all the property of those who were wealthy. And, after all, not all property is the gift of the Crown. My father's property, for example, has for the most part been amassed by himself and answers to his abilities. Should not able people, by right, retain the fruits of their abilities? And, so, shouldn't there be some other manner of suffrage than entirely equal for all?"

"This, indeed, is one of the fears of the wealthy," I would reply. "But what they leave out of consideration is that when a poor man attains property of his own he begins to respect property in general, the other person's as well as his. And, soon finding it necessary to protect his own property by law, he votes for such laws as will protect the other person's property also—even if larger than his. Only, of course, so long as the larger doesn't become behemoth and develop a taste for swallowing everyone's."

She would look at me very steadily, then say, "Perhaps. I must think about this more."

"And yet even this isn't the true fear of the wealthy," I would continue, pressing, insisting that she see more, that she see it as I did. "They only pretend to such a fear. Their true concern is to do away with all such restrictions as will hamper their free exploitation of everyone about them. This is the real cause for their opposing a general suffrage. And this is the true reason for its necessity."

"I must consider this further," she would respond, standing her ground. "I must think of it at length."

And under her knit brows her glance would continue to rest on me so steadily that it would preclude even the interference of a kiss.

On this morning she greeted me with a smile. "Your Sunday army seems to have trouble directing its feet," she said with mischievous good humor.

"They'll have no trouble sending their bullets home, if need be," I replied.

"You've never seen a regiment of the king's troops on parade," she exclaimed with more concern, as though trying to warn me. "The horse and the artillery and the foot, thousands of soldiers, all maneuvering on the same parade ground and all going as smoothly as the parts of a machine."

"Let's hope they try that pretty exercise when they're within firing range," I said. "But how did you find me?"

"Little Thomas. He and I are becoming fast friends."

"I'm so glad," I said. "It's I who taught him his letters and figures, you know. I think of him almost as a younger brother. He was born late to the people who own the inn."

"And I can see reflected in his eyes that I'm truly of some importance to you, which I must say is reassuring after your various disappearances. I've come to invite you to dinner this afternoon."

"I accept at once!"

"And be prepared to make an explanation to Father. The poor man has scarcely gotten over the tea dumping, and now he has heard about your army!"

As we talked, none other than Tommy himself came running along the road, hugging to his chest what looked like a bundle of newspapers.

"Jamie! Jamie!" he called. "These are for you from Mr. MacDougall."

He came up, with a gasp of relief handed me the roll of papers, and gave a quick smile to Elisabeth. "Mr. Mac-Dougall also says that the Sons committee will meet at two o'clock. And that Mr. Revere has arrived and will also be there."

Mention of Revere alerted me. Standing in the road I quickly scanned one journal after another.

They were English newspapers, just off ship, and their front pages blazoned Parliament's reply to Boston's tea dumping. I was thunderstruck! The port of Boston was declared closed to all commerce and was to remain closed till the town agreed to import taxed tea and to pay for the tea thrown into the harbor. Fundamental elements in the charter of Massachusetts as a self-governing colony were annulled. Virtually all her officials—councillors, judges, sheriffs, jurors—were to be appointed hereafter by the king's governor! Town meetings might be held only with his written permission! And to encourage His Majesty's soldiers in shooting down opposition, anyone arrested for murder while enforcing these edicts would be tried in England.

These measures, if successful, would kill the town of

77

Boston, indeed, destroy all Massachusetts, even destroy the patriot cause!

"Bad news, Jamie?"

I nodded.

I told Elisabeth the momentous information. "So I can't come to dinner this afternoon, after all. I must be at the Sons. Will you forgive me for staying away a while longer? Or perhaps I can visit later today."

She nodded soberly. "Later, then, today."

That afternoon there were no absentees from the Sons committee meeting.

"We must have your aid or we perish!" Revere exclaimed for the second or third time.

"We know that well."

"Then, damme, why do you hesitate! Why do you look at one another!"

"Because, good friend," replied MacDougall, "we do not possess the opinion of this colony as Sam Adams possesses that of Massachusetts. We are but a small portion here of those who may vote."

Revere's lips curved angrily in his honest, strong face. "Then what shall I tell Sam Adams?"

"That there lies before us a most desperate battle for the soul of New York."

The dispatch rider glared round at us, as though it were difficult for him to believe we all concurred.

"British troops will soon be sitting on our wharves and our commerce will be at an end," he cried. "A little while after that our tiny savings will be gone. And then our people will not have grain or meat to eat. Do you understand that?

How long afterward do you think it will be before we must submit?"

He could read sympathy upon our faces but not what Massachusetts wanted: a promise that New York would bar all commercial intercourse with England during the crisis— the same action which years before had so successfully brought England to terms in the Stamp Act dispute.

Revere recovered himself with an effort and extended his hand across the table, clasping that of MacDougall. "Forgive me my anger," he said. "We know your situation and your devotion to our cause and we could not ask for better men to forward the patriot policy."

We gave him a guide to show him the way to the river crossings that led to Philadelphia, and with the closing of the door behind him there began for us the struggle for New York.

"As swiftly as possible, before the faith of the various colonies in one another falls to pieces, we must force New York to act: to bar all English commerce from this colony so that New York does not batten while Boston dies. We must make it clear to England that the colonies are united; if she does not trade with one she may not trade with any. Meantime, of course, we will have to send money and food to Boston. For Revere said the truth when he warned they would face starvation in only a little while."

So spoke MacDougall.

"Yet the Colonial Assembly, which is filled with Royalists and Tories, will never adopt such measures," I observed unhappily.

"By a bold enough maneuver we may dispense with the Assembly," MacDougall said. "We already operate a tea watch in defiance of them. Why can't we call for the election of a committee at large to deal with the Boston crisis? Such a committee would not have to be illegal. We could consider it, rather, extralegal. If elected, as it rightly should be, from among all the people generally, who have already proved themselves so willing in the matter of the tea dumping, such a committee would be an instrument for adopting and enforcing a realistic, victorious policy."

It took me a moment to understand the profounder implications of the plan.

"We would, in effect, by ourselves and at one stroke, be enfranchising the people," I exclaimed. "We need only proclaim that all who wished to do so could vote for committee members!"

"Just so," replied MacDougall.

Behind the Kluger mansion a fine, large garden extended to the banks of the Hudson. It was beautifully landscaped with narrow, flagstoned pathways that wound about among the huge trunks of the primeval trees and led past alcoves with benches set so as to take advantage of the view over the river.

We sat in one of these alcoves, shielded from the rays of the setting sun by a high, curving hedge. Elisabeth listened wide-eyed with great excitement as I told her about Revere's visit.

"Father and his friends, too, have been talking about nothing but Boston," she said. "He feels somewhat as you do, that Boston ought in some way to be supported by us, but he is worried, he says, about the Sons of Liberty rousing the people to extreme actions. And I have some very interesting news for you. He thinks you might make a member of the Assembly."

"I?"

"Yes! Father thinks they might get the present Assembly dissolved and elect a new one, and in such a case he thinks the new elements in public opinion ought to be taken into account and some of their spokesmen endorsed. Oh, wouldn't it be wonderful, Jamie! You would be the Honorable James Hardy, member of the Colonial Assembly!"

"It would be wonderful in more ways than one," I said, reluctant to dampen her enthusiasm. "Stop and think. If the merchants make me a member of the Assembly, whose views would I be expected to champion—theirs or my own?"

"Why, the patriot view, I should imagine."

"But do you believe they would like it if I rose in the Assembly and demanded that all adult males be permitted to vote?"

"Oh, would you need to press that here and now? A general suffrage ought, perhaps, quite rightly to be one of the results of all our efforts, but couldn't it wait till after we've won our demands of England?"

"No. The merchants need us at just this moment and that gives us our leverage. After they've gained what they want from the British they'll merely continue to laugh slyly at us."

"Do you think they'd be as cynical as that?"

"Yes, my darling. Such is politics, because such is the constant, greedy, desperate scramble amongst groups for the wealth society produces."

Despite her interest in my argument, she seemed disappointed by my lack of interest in becoming a member of the Assembly. I felt sure there was little concern of her own here over place and status. I sensed, rather, that it had to do with her father—proving something about me to him.

I took both her hands in mine. "But the Assembly is already dead, really. The committee at large which I've told you the Sons will now propose will soon be the true ruling force in this city and on that committee I may well have a place. Wouldn't that do almost as well?"

"Yes, Jamie, of course it would!"

She gave me a small, almost sad smile, and I became certain that the whole matter of my being in the government was to impress her father; and that now she felt, perhaps apologetically, she had been too much influenced by this. I felt pained for the struggles being waged inside her.

I drew her close. And I marveled at the discovery that I was constantly following, or trying to follow, all that went on within her as intently as I tried to think out the reactions and moves of the politicians around me.

9.

"A DEVIL OF A TIME of day it is to call people to a meeting! Don't they know that Jack Jolt the carter and Tom Tapper the joiner have a livelihood to coin?"

"Brother patriot, I feel the same. One might even think they didn't want such as us here!"

Which was the very fact, I reflected, as I surveyed the crowded scene while lending half an ear to the two fellows beside me.

The idea of a newly elected extralegal committee to deal with the Boston crisis in place of the Tory Assembly must have been in the very air. For the merchants, too, had decided to adopt the device. And, interested as they were in only a small segment of the population, which did not have to be organized or educated as did the greater mass of the people, they were able to act on the instant and send out their call before ours.

Cleverly, they had set the time for their public meeting at half past two, so that mainly those who were their own masters in business matters could take time off to attend. Broadcloths and ruffles far outnumbered plain wool.

Yet the spirit of the town was such that more persons were continually arriving and the press in the Exchange kept growing ever greater.

The Exchange itself was an odd structure fashioned like a Greek temple. Instead of exterior walls, classic columns supported its pedimented roof. On its two long sides the building was actually open to the street through these colonnades and was thus fairly well suited to a popular gathering.

In the center of the stone-paved floor a platform had been improvised of planks laid across barrels, and upon this, Isaac Low, the wealthy and conservative Dock Street merchant, now mounted.

"Dear friends," he announced. "The distress visited upon Boston is causing us all the gravest concern. The spectacle of our sister colony embroiled in strife with our parent government moves us profoundly. To exhibit indifference is to confess a callousness which, I am certain, is not truly of our nature.

"A group of public-spirited and responsible men among us has been prompted by these considerations to call you together so that we may consult with one another. They have done me the honor to nominate me, temporarily, the chairman of this gathering. And perhaps our very first action should be to choose a permanent chairman. I shall now throw the floor open to such nominations."

At once, from near the platform, the young John Jay, slender and dark and famed for his precocious legal attainments, raised his hand, and upon being recognized, called forth, "Mr. Low, I place your own name in nomination."

James Duane, also a lawyer, and also of the conservative persuasion, seconded.

I wondered whether MacDougall or Lamb would nominate one of the Sons. But no other name was offered. They must have decided that given the nature of the attendance we stood only to suffer a defeat. Low was declared chairman.

"I will take but a moment from our business," he said, "to express my appreciation of the honor bestowed on me and to assure you I am fully cognizant of the responsibilities entailed. And now, I believe, Mr. Haynes of Pearl Street has a communication to make. Mr. Haynes?"

"I have a proposal, Mr. Low, as to how the citizens of this town may best make their attitudes felt. The times are become so critical that the attention of citizens to events is now required almost constantly. Yet we cannot come to meetings every day. And so it has occurred to me, as it has to others of my fellow citizens, that we ought to appoint a standing committee from among us to watch over affairs. Some of us have gone so far in this matter as to draw up a list of names of those we feel should serve on this committee. If you will all do me the kindness to listen I shall read off this list for your consideration and then put this proposal in the form of a motion for you to approve or disapprove."

I listened intently as he read his names—and swore an oath under my breath. For of the twenty-five men he named, no fewer than ten were out-and-out Tories: despisers of "mobocracy," as they put it, and adulators of the protecting Crown and its "prerogatives." And of the remainder, most were known to be so grasping that they could not in the slightest be depended upon to deny themselves the extra profits to be made from Boston's immobility.

"I feel sure you will appreciate the common sense here compacted," Haynes went on. "This is a group which will examine issues without fanaticism and will act without rashness. These men represent the weighty interests of our colony—landholders, importers, shipowners, those who sell at wholesale. It is a group which inspires confidence!"

To my indignation, "Aye"s and "Indeed"s rang out on all sides.

"May we have a second to the motion nominating this committee so that it may be discussed in proper form and then put to a vote?" Low requested.

"Mr. Chairman," called out Peter Wallis, another merchant, "I deem it a privilege so to second."

"Mr. Chairman," called a keen, rasping voice, "I ask the floor."

"The chair recognizes Mr. John Lamb."

Lamb was standing near the front of the gathering. He now turned his back upon the platform and, ruddy with anger, addressed the assemblage.

"Mr. Chairman and fellow citizens, the main business of this meeting should not be to elect a committee but to answer Boston's cry for help. The means of livelihood has just been denied that great port by a most vicious kind of retaliation. She now asks that we support her: that we cease immediately our own trade with England. Once before, these colonies combined to refuse to import all English goods, and the blow struck England so forcefully that it quickly brought about the repeal of the Stamp Act. All here remember the occasion. We must do the same again.

86

"But will the committee that has just been nominated adopt any such policy? Of course not. No one here today can possibly believe that these self-seeking merchants will bring themselves to cut off their own trade with England in order to help Boston. Quite to the contrary. I fear that using various delays, subterfuges, and excuses, they will seize the opportunity to augment their profits and to enhance their trading position.

"I wish to offer a countercommittee, and all who recognize the names on it will recognize also that they are the names of men who will adopt a straightforward policy in support of Boston. Boston's struggle is none other than our own. The Sons of Liberty warn: If Boston falls, unsupported and alone, so will we all at the last fall, one by one and alone."

From a sheet of paper he began calling off his names. Even as he went along cries of "No!" and "Never!" rose from the crowd.

After the list had been seconded, Fleming Craddock, a silverware importer from Pearl Street, asked for the floor.

"Mr. Chairman and fellow citizens," he said, "it is with trepidation and dread that I have heard the names suggested by Mr. Lamb. His is a committee of levelers and godless men, of disdainers of law and destroyers of property, just such as those who so hastily destroyed the tea in Boston and brought the present calamities upon that town. In our own colony they have already succeeded in placing New York, too, within the shadow of the king's retribution. Shall we now go ahead and make certain that the threatening disaster falls upon us by giving over the conduct of affairs to them?"

Approving "Hear, hear"s arose and applause started up.

I asked for the floor.

"Gentlemen," I said, trying to keep my voice unimpassioned and hoping to convince by force of argument, "New York is one of the two great ports at the center of the chain of colonies. Together with Philadelphia, it is their commercial linchpin. It behooves us therefore to think in terms of all these colonies, of the entire continent. The Tories and narrow, grasping men who in such large part compose Mr. Haynes' ticket are incapable of seeing beyond their own purses. They will inevitably fasten upon the 'practical' policy, and through their control of the key colony of New York they will sink the entire patriot cause. I beg you to encompass this truth."

Cries again swept the assemblage, this time expressing annoyance and impatience. "To the vote! To the vote!"

When Mr. Haynes' list was presented the heavy swell of "Aye"'s indicated clearly enough that the great majority held for the merchants. Only a small number valiantly shouted "Aye" for the Sons' list.

Mr. Low announced, "I declare Mr. Haynes' committee to be elected and to be henceforth the true organ of the opinion of the people of this town. And I am sure I speak for the entire committee when, as one of its members, I promise you we shall devote the utmost attention to the problem confronting us. And now, unless anyone feels he has an additional matter of major importance to present, I will entertain a motion to adjourn."

Through the dispersing crowd Lamb, MacDougall, Willett, Sears, other Sons committeemen, and myself pushed toward one another and formed an angry group at one side of the building.

There we were approached by Isaac Low, John Jay,

Martin Kluger, James Duane, and Philip Livingston of the merchants' party.

"God guide us all, gentlemen," Low said soberly. "We trust you take some share, at least, in our satisfaction with the action of the citizenry?"

"Not one whit!" spat out Lamb.

"What? Even though the choice was made in the democratical manner you so constantly advocate?"

"A semblance of the manner was there, but a semblance only, for the meeting was packed by trickery. We will show you by the size of the public meeting the Sons shall now proceed to call which of our factions has the better right to speak for the citizenry. And then we will show you by the strength of our watch along the wharves and by the spirit of our military formations which of our factions is the more capable of enforcing its attitudes."

Philip Livingston, of the merchants' group, tall, thin, with an easy stoop and a habitually sardonic expression on his bony face, pushed to their fore.

"Gentlemen," he said, turning to his colleagues, "it appears we have won too great a victory and are about to lose the entire game by it. I have a suggestion to make."

The merchants bent upon him looks of indignation, yet remained attentive, for he had long proved himself one of their acutest thinkers. Livingston was a strange man: a wealthy merchant, scion of one of the most powerful families in the colony, yet a lone hunter with a touch of something desperate about him and sympathies that were at times surprisingly democratic.

"I suggest that we all repair to my residence and there sit down and talk out the difference between us until we arrive at a *modus operandi.* I suggest, indeed, that unless we do

89

just this our two factions will fall into such a struggle as will end either in the disaster of a great victory for the Sons of Liberty or in the disaster of the exhaustion of both factions and a complete victory, at the last, for British policy."

"I think we'd best do something of the sort," Martin Kluger agreed.

Livingston arched his eyebrows inquiringly toward the other merchants. For the most part they murmured agreement. Then he turned to us.

"Yes, we'll come with you," said MacDougall.

Livingston nodded appreciatively. He led the way down to the Bowling Green, and in five minutes we were on the side of the little park, opposite the Klugers', where stood the Livingston house.

Inside the entry servants took our hats and cloaks and then Livingston led us upstairs to a large music room—to judge by the harpsichord—that was brightly lighted by many windows. Servants carried in additional chairs, set out Madeira and rum, and offered about pipe coals.

When we were settled MacDougall rose and said, "I must state without any equivocation that the Sons cannot possibly accept the newly elected committee as it is now constituted. Fully a third are Tories determined in advance to leave Boston to her fate and the rest will for the most part abet them. This will not bear further discussion. You must understand that the Sons of Liberty will never abandon Boston."

Out of the silence left to the merchants came the composed voice of John Jay. "I agree with you as to the attitudes of the committee, and I believe my colleagues will agree, too, after reflection. But you must recognize a premise equally fundamental to ourselves, which is that

New York cannot undertake, by herself and without hearing from the other colonies, a policy of total embargo of British goods. We, too, would only be losing our trade to the other ports."

Willett spoke up for the Sons. "Were New York at least to initiate a move in this direction, demonstrating sincerity, the other colonies would be emboldened to follow suit. We think we must take the chance. Let us show the way."

"A chance is all it would be," returned Jay. "The realistic condition with which we must reckon is that we cannot rely on the merchants of, say, Philadelphia, who are also interested in enlarging their profits, to follow such a lead any more than the Sons of Liberty of New York trust their own merchants to support such a policy."

We had apparently escaped a deadlock over the membership of the new committee only to approach a deadlock on the more fundamental issue of an embargo against British goods.

Almost simultaneously, it seemed, everyone sensed the way out.

Isaac Low said, "If we could induce all the colonies to embargo trade with Britain at one and the same time, I suppose that would be a stroke of policy!"

He spoke diffidently and hesitantly. Behind such a view there was implied a general congress of all the colonies. And that was a possibility he and his colleagues approached with great apprehension. For in such a congress the radicals of Virginia and South Carolina—the Lees and Patrick Henrys and Gadsdens—would join forces with the radicals of Massachusetts—the Adamses and Hancocks and Warrens— and united, they might well dominate the proceedings.

Lamb exclaimed with great emphasis, "Such unity among

91

the colonies is exactly what we feel must eventually be achieved! We will forego pressing for an embargo by this colony alone, or for a committee entirely to our taste, if you will join us in issuing a call for a continent-wide congress— just such a congress as was called so successfully to consider the Stamp Act nine years ago."

The merchants looked at one another uneasily. And to do them justice I think they no longer feared the loss of great profits so much as they did the firebrands of Virginia and Massachusetts.

John Jay again spoke up.

"I, for one, endorse the idea of a continental congress. I think our differences with England are very deep and we stand in great danger of subjection and abject exploitation. If this be so, we must find a device whereby all the colonies may act together."

Another pause followed, allowing for thought among the reluctant merchants.

"Well, then," said Low at last, "do I understand it to be the sense of this gathering that we reply to Boston by proposing to our sister colonies a congress of all of us which shall suggest policy for all?"

There were nods and several sighs, but no objections.

These solid men of commerce and of order were putting their feet on a road that connected with the highway to revolution, and they felt it. To call for a congress of all the colonies was next door to raising a central government—a central organ whose control might be seized by those they considered hotheads.

"Now," said MacDougall, "I believe we can return to the question of the new committee's composition."

The discussion that followed was brief and overshadowed

by the new concept of a continental congress. In short order a different committee was chosen. Its cast remained conservative but it was a committee we could more hopefully expect to act for the patriot cause, even if it dragged its feet. And it was agreed, at our insistence, that this new list—the Committee of Fifty-One, as it should henceforth be called—would be ratified by a vote of the people at large.

Then we returned to the question of a continental congress and chose John Jay, on account of his legal abilities and his fine literary style, to write the letter of suggestion to Boston.

Philip Livingston rose and raised his glass. "To a continental congress, gentlemen!"

We all rose. "To a continental congress!"

10.

August 1774

TWO MILES ABOVE THE TOWN, along the highway that led down to us from New England, the first and second New York volunteer militia companies waited, a single file on each side of the road.

Though we boasted no uniforms, I felt we presented a spectacle that would have won approval from the officers of any professional army in the world. Each man's hair was neatly caught at the back of his neck; each wore a hunting shirt held in at the waist by a belt from which hung a powder flask and bullet pouch; and each grasped the barrel of a newly furbished musket which rested, most properly, butt on the ground beside his right foot.

A mounted lookout appeared at last around a bend up the road and waved excitedly at us; and very shortly there came into view behind him the coach we expected.

I called the command "Present arms!" and the vehicle rolled forward between two lines of smart-looking soldiery.

At the end of our formation there waited on horseback MacDougall, Lamb, Willett, Low, Livingston, Kluger, and others, and now they spurred their horses out into the middle of the highway. The coach halted, its doors swung open, hands came out to be shaken, smiling faces appeared at the windows, and the militia fired volley after volley.

Then, at a signal from MacDougall, I gave the order to face forward and march, and the entire party moved in the direction of town, the horsemen riding on each side of the coach and the militia marching one company before it and one company behind.

I knew full well that Sam Adams must be one of the men in the coach. I kept falling back to inspect the marching column more often than was needful in the hope of discerning which one might be he. But the interior was dark and the five men within fairly crowded it. The parade entered the town and came to a halt before Hull's, where we had arranged for the delegation to stay, and still I had not made out which of the delegates was Sam Adams.

Lamb and the other committeemen ushered the arrivals into their quarters while I attended to dismissing the militia. Then Marinus Willett came out of the inn bearing a list of some twenty figures in the town who were to be invited to confer with the Massachusetts delegates to the Continental Congress. I was to select messengers and arrange for the delivery of the invitations.

This I accomplished within the next hour or so while suffering the keenest disappointment at not having seen Sam Adams. It seemed I was quite superfluous just where I wanted most to be present.

Luckily, there was someplace else where I was as welcome as I could wish. For it was Sunday and I was to see Elisabeth, as had become our custom on Sundays.

*　　*　　*

Elisabeth was in the garden in one of our favorite alcoves. She wore a new gown made of silk cloth from Cathay, golden yellow with black markings that looked like signs in the mysterious alphabet of that land. The bright color set off her warm complexion while the black characters matched her eyes.

Those eyes were now warm and alert with sympathy.

"You have brought your precious Sam Adams safely into town?"

"Yes. He's ensconced at Hull's, with the rest."

"What's the matter? Has he turned out other than you expected?"

"The fact is, I haven't met him, and I'm not even sure which of the group he is, or what he looks like." And I told her about the welcoming parade.

"It seems rather a small thing to disappoint you so," she said, putting her hand up to my cheek.

"But you don't understand who he is. It is Sam Adams who leads the opposition to England throughout the whole chain of the colonies. We consider him our chief, though we do not acknowledge him such by any sign. And he has maintained this captaincy for almost a decade, now, by the brilliance of his ideas and by great force of character. It is he who conceived the nonimportation concept by which the colonies forced the repeal of the Stamp Act. And it is he who directed every step of the maneuvers which ended with Boston's tea dumping. Patriot leaders in each colony ponder every word he writes, be it private correspondence or public pamphlet or article for a gazette, and from these they take the cues for many of their own actions."

"I see," said Elisabeth. "But there still remains time. Father says the delegates will stop in New York at least two days more. In fact, Father is to meet with them sometime tomorrow, with several of the other merchants."

"I know," I said. "I myself arranged to deliver the invitations. But I won't be there."

As we spoke, Tommy came down the path toward our alcove, looking about him. Upon catching sight of us he broke into a run. Elisabeth's welcoming arm closed round him in a hug.

"Mr. MacDougall sends you this," he said to me, pulling out an envelope from beneath his shirt.

The note was brief. "Sam Adams wishes to meet in secrecy with the most devoted of the Sons. Will your lodging at the Spread Sail be available for such a gathering —tonight at nine, about eleven people, yourself included. Reply by same messenger. Destroy."

I tore the note into bits. "Tell Mr. MacDougall yes."

"And tell Louisa to give you one of the oranges which we have just received from Barbary," Elisabeth said. "You must tear off the skin before eating it. Ask Louisa to show you."

When he was gone I kissed Elisabeth and rose. "I must be off without delay."

"But you've only just arrived!"

"It's the note. Something very important—and very secret. I can't tell you, my darling."

She gazed at me without saying a word, a neutral, steady gaze.

"I can't," I repeated, beginning to feel a bit desperate until she smiled. Then, "But this much I'll say, for I know by now you keep my secrets. It has to do with Sam Adams."

Since I was eleven years old my lodging at the Spread Sail Inn had been the chamber in the attic.

It was a low-ceilinged room, with roof beams sweeping down to less than a man's height at the outer walls, but comfortably spacious and well lighted. It occupied half the length of the uppermost story and boasted three windows along one side and another at the rear gable end which looked out over the river. By day it was cheerfully bright, and at night the heavens with the stars and the varying moon came down wondrously close. It was a splendid room in which to have grown up.

This chamber had also the advantage of great privacy in that it was reached by an outside stairway which climbed up the rear of the inn, on the river side. No doubt this was the factor MacDougall had in mind in calling a secret meeting here. The stairway had been added to facilitate the operations of the inn, for the attic was used also as a storeroom; and all around me on the flooring outside my chamber, in their season, were drying apples, cured meats, preserves, and a host of other commodities, mingling their odors into a piquant-sweet essence.

The furnishings in my room were few but sufficient: a cot under the river-side window; at the opposite end a writing table and chair, with a bookcase; and in a corner on the blind wall a washstand. Farther along the same wall was a fireplace, and at the side of this stood another table and two more chairs.

With the help of one of the inn servants, I brought up additional chairs which I arranged in an oval, and the room was ready for a meeting.

Shortly thereafter the guests began to arrive. First to enter, accompanied by Isaac Sears, was Thomas Cushing, of medium height, self-possessed and determined-looking. After him, with Marinus Willett, came John Hancock, a slender, tall man in his forties, elegantly appareled and with fine little mannerisms, almost like those of a dandy. Escorted by Lamb was John Adams, the famous young Boston lawyer and cousin to Sam Adams, a vibrant, quick-eyed man with a large, round head and a decisive bearing. The very last to enter were Alexander MacDougall and Sam Adams.

"I am pleased to meet you," said Adams in a simple manner, shaking my hand and looking me full in the face. He appeared to be in his middle fifties, spare and of medium height. He wore a plain brown suit and his voice had something of a minister's or orator's dry depth to it.

He glanced about the room and then at MacDougall.

MacDougall said, "We are all here. Do you wish the door locked?"

"Not necessarily. But it would be well to keep a keen eye upon it."

We settled ourselves in the chairs, the New Englanders on one side, and the New Yorkers on the other.

Sam Adams, in the center of the New Englanders, was tacitly accepted as the directing head of the meeting. His straight, brown hair, I now saw, was streaked with gray. His somewhat longish face was lined and thoughtful, and his large black eyes were strikingly luminous.

One by one, unhurriedly, he surveyed the men on the New York side. Then he spoke.

"I have asked Alexander MacDougall, on peril of all our lives, to invite here tonight only those leaders of the New York Sons of whose devotion and discretion he is utterly certain."

MacDougall spoke up, his usual forcefulness curbed somewhat by deference. "And so have I done."

"The matter I shall broach will place the necks of all who hear me in the noose. I therefore beg, even at this late moment, that if there be any present who cannot accept such risk, they rise and leave. No censure will attach to those who retire, and I ask only that they keep silence about what they have already heard."

No man stirred.

"Gentlemen, what I have to propose is that from this moment onward we strive for nothing less than independence."

The New Englanders on either side of him sat motionless but scrutinizing us all.

"Beyond this point, to continue the struggle merely in order to preserve our rights within the framework of the British constitution must lead to failure and enslavement. British courts must always, on all overriding issues, uphold the acts of Parliament; British troops will support both; and the ministry's action against Boston makes the future, in this respect, all too clear."

It thrilled me so greatly to hear the signal at long last given for independence that I could scarcely follow what else was said.

"If we throw in our lot for independence we will unlock the enthusiastic energies of the broadest stratum of the people; and at the same time we will create the possibility of military support from France or Holland."

MacDougall said, "You consider, then, that these colonies have a military potential capable of winning independence?"

"Very close to it, at the least. And with the aid of the French or Dutch, beyond question."

"I, too, hope for French support," said Lamb, "but I have

doubts whether a despotic monarchy will aid levelers and republicans."

"I have doubts also," said Adams, "but we must wager it. I am hoping that to the French the eventual possibility of unrestricted commerce with North America will outweigh the other considerations."

Adams' calm, all-encompassing gaze had become a challenge to which reply was now imperative.

MacDougall said, "We of the New York Sons of Liberty are with you, shoulder to shoulder, at every step of the way, and, if need be, to the death."

Adams rose and extended his hand to MacDougall. All at once and spontaneously the two delegations arose and excitedly and fervently shook hands.

When we resumed our chairs I felt that we were not quite the same men; that we had just sailed through a most difficult strait, on the other side of which the waters and shores were new and strange and without known limit.

Adams resumed. "At the Continental Congress to which we go I shall in various ways, and however suitable, urge this course on the others. I already feel sure that much of the South will follow us. But the middle colonies are weak, weakest of all being your own New York. You realize that without New York we are but a broken body—we are militarily divided and defeated in advance. Alexander MacDougall, New York must not fail us."

"What human effort can do, we will do," MacDougall answered.

Adams went on. "Tomorrow we meet with your merchants. As you may well imagine, the discussion will be different from this. I shall try to assuage their fears of what they consider our impetuousness and merely urge them to a somewhat more forward course. Revolution and independence are considerations only for those of us who are at this moment in this room. And, having made our minds clear to one another, I beg you to keep our views in the utmost secrecy until such time as we are able to show our hand."

He rose. "The hour is late for New Englanders, dear friends. We will say good night."

We all got up and shook hands again. I led the way down the rear staircase to the yard, and in small groups and by different routes we guided the New Englanders back to Hull's.

11.

"IT'S REGRETTABLE that we've had so few intimate dinners, Jamie," Kluger commented.

"I agree, sir," I replied.

Elisabeth clapped her hands with delight at the success of her arrangement. "Oh, I shall plan many more of them!"

The three of us were still seated around the small table in the dining room where we had enjoyed dinner.

"Yes. We are apt to lose touch in the hurly-burly of events," Kluger went on. His expression became somewhat abstracted and then a little grim. "You've heard about the Suffolk Resolves?"

"Oh, Papa!" Elisabeth exclaimed. "Today, let's leave politics for later!"

"I fear me the Massachusetts gentry are setting the stage at Philadelphia for nothing less than revolt, my dear," Kluger went on.

"Jamie and I have very important matters to discuss with you, Papa."

Kluger glanced sharply at her and then at me, and continued to lecture her on the Suffolk Resolves.

"The county which surrounds Boston has just delivered itself of a most violent set of resolutions. They declare that the king has forfeited the allegiance of the colonies; that the act of Parliament which destroys the Massachusetts charter is itself null and void; and that the towns of that province should choose militia officers, arm themselves, and seize the Crown's officers as hostages, if need be."

"Jamie and I have talked about that at length," Elisabeth responded patiently.

"Which is by no means the worst of it," Kluger went on irritably, as though she had not spoken. "They have now presented these Resolves to the Congress at Philadelphia for endorsement. And if Sam Adams succeeds in forcing them down the throat of that body, why, we are all as good as convicted rebels! Who knows but that wily old Adams wrote the Resolves himself and set the time for their passage before ever he left Boston!"

"He's a very capable politician, of course," I answered in as neutral a voice as I could muster. It was not that I feared to espouse the wonderful Resolves. I had something more personal and pressing to discuss.

"Sir," I began hesitantly—and continued not at all. My mouth became dry and my face warm. I managed to resume somewhat obliquely, "As you may have guessed, Elisabeth and I have—in the past several months we have—"

"Have been seeing a great deal of each other," Kluger completed for me, "and find each other desirable."

"Yes, sir," I said. "And now we would like—should like—perhaps I should say are taking under serious consideration—"

"Becoming affianced and married," Kluger again finished off for me.

"Yes, sir."

Kluger raised his wine glass to his face and looked at it. He said to Elisabeth, "He speaks for you as well, I take it?"

"Oh, yes, Papa," she said, taking my hand.

Kluger studied the space between us. "My own interest, naturally, is to see that my daughter makes a happy marriage. And I believe I am aware of some of the factors that enter into that for her. But I'm not at all sure that you and she are aware of what they may be."

He lowered the glass to the table and turned squarely to me. "For example, Hardy, your character and your ability are to my mind all that can be desired. But you are a mechanic—a shipwright—almost a journeyman. Do you think my daughter has the tastes and background for being made happy on the earnings of a shipwright?"

"Oh, Papa," Elisabeth cried, "Jamie won't remain a shipwright all his life. I'm sure he'll rise and rise and you'll be very proud of him."

"Will he indeed rise?" Kluger asked. "I would be most happy to see him rise. I'll go further and say that I am willing to make a place for him in my own enterprises. In fact I'll put the question to him here and now: Jamie, will you consider accepting a position with me?"

"Well, sir," I replied, "I can't at this very moment desert my shipwrights and the political influence they give me, together with the goals they help me strive toward, in order to embark on a purely personal career. As you know, I hope to see certain changes made in society, and I feel very much responsible for helping bring them about. Once they're achieved, however, perhaps I can think about more personal responsibilities."

"And how long do you think it will be before such changes are effected—if ever they really are?"

"Perhaps a year, perhaps two. Probably not over three years at the outermost."

"Then let's defer the question of your marriage to Elisabeth until that period—that brief period, to hear you tell it—is over, and we can all see more clearly where we stand."

I looked at him with astonishment. "Time is one thing as it's reckoned for public events, and very much another as it's reckoned for personal relationships. Three years in public affairs is a brief interval. But three years for Elisabeth and me to wait is a very long period."

Kluger turned to his daughter. "And you, Elisabeth, do you feel the same way?"

"Yes, Papa, I do," she replied.

"And suppose you and Jamie are married, say, within the year. How will the two of you live? Will you move to his room at the Spread Sail and cook for him and wash and sew? I think you might, for the shortest romantic while—for you're a girl of spirit. But in my opinion it wouldn't last six months that way and I'll not consent to it. No, I will allow no marriage in which Elisabeth fails to be maintained in decency and comfort."

Elisabeth was taken aback. Caught between Kluger's emphatic "No," so obviously out of concern for her happiness, and his reasonable-seeming offer of a solution— my accepting a position with him—she hesitated. She turned to me.

"Jamie, don't you think it possible, after all is considered, that you might join with Father now? The cause of the shipwrights—of all our people—seems well launched.

Aren't there other leaders able to take up for them? And for the larger consideration, defending ourselves against Britain, is not Father—aren't we all—on the same patriot side?"

I understood her better at the moment than she understood herself. I understood her great love and admiration for her father; his dominance over her; her inability at this particular instant to set herself four-square against him.

My love, my insight, provided balm for the indignation that cut through me.

I tried to match, in tone at least, Kluger's own apparent reasonableness. "It may be possible, yes. Give me some time to think, to see whether I can come to terms with myself about it."

"You must understand, though, Jamie," Kluger went on, "my politics lie where my commercial activities lie. They further them. But your politics are an outgrowth of your idealism. I oppose the British because the monopolies they're granting their own merchants threaten to destroy me. You oppose them because you want to experiment with bestowing all sorts of rights and privileges on the unpropertied. In the long run that entails attacking me, also.

"Before I could let you enter my organization I should have to be sure that you were engaged in politics the same way I am and along with me—to protect and further my interests. Would you be willing to make such a change?"

"Why, you would have me turn renegade to the principles I live by!" I exclaimed.

Kluger shrugged. "Don't you see I have to ask you to make such a choice? It would be folly to introduce into my affairs a young man who would use his abilities to obstruct and injure them. This is the merest common sense of life."

I was struck dumb with an agony of frustration. Rage at

107

his standing in my way fought within me against a realization of something of the justice in what he said, at least from his point of view. And yet my heart cried out: What has all this to do with me and Elisabeth?

Kluger added, "You don't have to make up your mind this very day. But before I can possibly consent to Elisabeth's marrying you, you will have to be earning enough to make her comfortable. And if you want to marry her at once, I see no other immediate source of such income for you than a position in my own enterprises—to have which you must accommodate yourself to my views."

"But you may be so wrong! Both of you!" Elisabeth's eyes were blazing now. "The matter cannot be so clear-cut and simple as the two of you would have it!"

Her voice was passionate, emphatic, resolute. I had never before heard it so.

"You men! You fighting cocks! Ever ready at a moment to square away and begin to cannonade! Can you really see no other solution?"

Kluger turned to her, clearly surprised. He replied heavily, "No, I cannot, my dear, and it is by my own years and experience that my judgment must abide."

Not faltering for a moment Elisabeth turned sharply to me. "And you, Jamie?" she demanded.

"How can I turn upon the principles by which I see all right and wrong—that I have labored with the needs of my inmost soul to make clear to you—in order to enter a counting house and there sell them off for money!"

"Now, mark me, Father," she said, turning upon Kluger again. "There is something you must know at once. And that is that I have come to understand and in great measure

108

to agree with Jamie's concern for people at large—for those who make up this world. That little boy Tommy whom you see bringing me Jamie's messages, those lads and fathers I have come to know on the tea watch and in Jamie's militia, they have every right—yes, every duty—to rise to their own greatest possible heights as human beings. For this, they all must have an education—that raising of the eyes all about one that tells one who one is—paid for, if need be, by taxes on that sacred property of yours, which will by no means impoverish you. They must have their own plot of land, of which there is more than sufficient for all in this new world. And most important, to guard themselves against great whales that drive the seas with open maw and swallow everything before them, they must each and all have the right to vote—their word in the management of affairs."

Some of the words and phrases were my own. But the understanding, the conviction, were all hers.

Kluger stared and stared. At last he said, "And now that you, too, are a leveler, I take it that you are prepared to throw away all I have—all *we* have?"

"Of course not," she replied ringingly. "I say there is enough in this land for everyone. Nor need it be parceled out in the same measure for each. But each must have at the least his birthright—the right to be secure in those things that are needful for him to grow up in God's own image."

She turned to me, grasping my hand where it lay on the table, and took us both in now, still with the most marvelous mixture of fire and drive. "It is only the willful, stubborn pride in all you men of extraordinary capacity, your wish to have everything go your own way and no other, that makes you draw such adamant, opposing lines. But it is my hope to have both of you—the father I love and the man I love! And for this you must each of you find your way in some part toward the other."

With smoldering eyes, Kluger glared out of a set, darkening face at Elisabeth. Addressing himself to me, though looking at his daughter, he grated out, "You don't have to make up your mind this very day, Hardy. But it remains as I have said: before I consent to Elisabeth's marrying you, you'll have to be able to provide for her properly. And if that is by joining me you'll have to see your way clear to supporting my own attitudes. And please remember—should she choose to set her foot down, she has relatives in the West Indies, where I can always send her till her infatuation for you passes."

12.

UNTIL THAT EVENING'S TALK I had been an idealistic young man happily engaged in furthering the progress of mankind, or so I thought, and had given little thought to my own selfish ends. Freedom for our people from without—from Europe's tyrannies—was what I strove after, and safeguarding against similar tyrannies that might develop from within. The aims were clear and high-minded and the struggle had its own exhilarating rewards, for it was elevating and inspiring.

Ruefully, now, I realized that my selflessness had been somewhat easily come by. There was little I had been called upon to sacrifice in order to pursue such a course. There was virtually nothing I had stood to lose thereby.

Now, however, I stood to lose indeed. Now I stood to make sacrifices for my views. And I was mortified to learn how unready I was.

Elisabeth's slim form and dark eyes on one side of the scale weighed it down at once and heavily. Nor was that all. Wealth, too, might be mine for the abandonment of my freight of principle. For the first time in my life I sensed almost physically how it could mean release from the day's long effort in the shipyard or some similar toil, and how it supported an urbane way of living which would, in any case, have to go along with Elisabeth, if I was realistically to take her happiness into consideration.

And on the other side of the scale? My hope that sometime in the future, after there had been achieved the great things for which I labored—freedom from England, suffrage for mechanics, farms for those who wanted them, education for all—the people might flower out to fulfill my expectations of them. Ephemeral, yet wonderful.

And I understood how deeply Elisabeth loved her father; that even if we managed to evade him, to elope and marry, there would always remain a part of her heart deeply wounded with anguish on his account.

What, now, of the idealistic magnanimity with which I strove after elevating the lot of the people at large? Was it to become, with its self-righteous rejection of any compromise, an instrument of permanent unhappiness for the girl I so much loved?

My dilemma pressed on me constantly, and my preoccupation with it created a screen, night and day, between myself and whatever business I had in hand.

Standing above the town in the pasturages where we fed and rested the cattle that passed through on their way to succor Boston, I would be conversing with the herdsmen.

"It might break out into open conflict after all—into warfare," I suggested to one such drover who had come the distance from the Carolina frontier. He was tall and gaunt, with sun-darkened skin stretched tautly over his cheekbones, and his powerful frame was all sinew and bone.

112

Quite like an Indian he was arrayed in traveling dress of shirt, breeches, and moccasins, all of deerskin.

"My grandfather fell at Culloden Moor," he replied, "and my father was hunted through the Highlands for years after. I'll not be hunted here."

He handled his musket as casually as a walking stick and his light blue eyes rested on my face as easily as though he had just told me the time of day. And as his silence continued I realized this was all he intended to say and that his reply was meant to cover any and all contingencies.

Along the frontier from Pennsylvania to Georgia there were Scotch-Irish such as he, determined to retain the freedom they had sought so passionately; and when I thought of the spirit of these backwoodsmen conjoined with that of our town mechanics my heart overflowed with reassurance.

Then Kluger's ultimatum returned to the forefront of my thoughts. Were I to join his party I might well have to help filch from men like these their birthrights—to have a say in affairs, to be able to defend their modest property, to see that their children went to school.

Or was that a true presentation of alternatives? Was it not too dramatically sharpened and opposed, as befitted better the mind of a propagandist? Might not Kluger's cautious views evolve at long last in the very same direction as those of the Sons?

Or, again, were such second thoughts only clever efforts to gull myself into accepting the price Kluger demanded for Elisabeth?

I was becoming confused.

*　　*　　*

Enwrapped in such thoughts, I was walking along Water Street, inspecting the tea watch, when Tommy ran up.

"Alexander MacDougall says for you to be at Philip Livingston's house at four o'clock. Mr. Jay will be there."

Jay? Jay was supposed to be in Philadelphia, where he was a delegate to the Continental Congress.

"I'll be there, Tommy."

At the Livingstons' the manservant showed me straightaway up the stairs to the music room and I saw that an emergency meeting of the new Committee of Fifty-One had been called. I took my seat with MacDougall and the others of the Sons. Out of the corner of my eye, across the room, I saw that Kluger was present, too, and he seemed to me a figure out of a dream or nightmare with whom, I suddenly remembered, I had unfinished business.

When it appeared that almost the entire Committee of Fifty-One had arrived, John Jay rose and took up a position beside the marble mantelpiece.

"My friends and colleagues in the patriot cause," he began. "I trust you will permit me to dispense with the trappings of formal address and pass directly to the matter which has brought me from Philadelphia.

"A question with profound implications has just been placed before the delegates at the Continental Congress, one which to my mind embodies grave dangers—sufficient for me to return in order to sound out your opinions and ask your advice.

"The Continental Congress is now considering the particular form in which an embargo against English commerce might best be put into effect. It is a plan which those who advocate it call 'the Association.'

"In brief, they intend that in every town, city, and county

there should be chosen a committee to observe the conduct of all the citizens; and with respect to those who fail to adhere to such an embargo, to seize their goods and to enforce a breaking off of all relations with them by the others in the community. The citizenry would be asked to sign petitions saying that they 'associate' themselves to do these things.

"Now, bring to mind, gentlemen, the tremendous meaning of this. For two men to come together and agree not to purchase English goods is an action rightfully theirs. But for these two men to decide that if a third man does not agree with them they may destroy his property and ostracize him is something very different. In the first instance we have a peaceable effort on the part of citizens to make a protest. In the second instance we have the assumption of coercive, of governmental, powers.

"Now, too, please recall, gentlemen, that the Continental Congress was created as a consultative and advisory body. To vote a policy of nonintercourse which is to be enforced in this manner is subtly but most definitely to create, instead, a new center of governmental power.

"As background to my concern it is only needful for you to bear in mind that these powers would be in the hands of a Congress which has turned so radical in its views as to have endorsed and adopted the Suffolk Resolves."

As Jay paused to drink from a glass on the mantelpiece, there was a stir and a murmur among his hearers, a shaking of heads among the more cautious of the merchants.

When he had refreshed himself, Jay resumed. "This is the substance of what I have to place before you. Perhaps, now, I'd best hear your opinions."

Alexander MacDougall spoke up.

"Gentlemen, it seems to me our young friend stresses unduly the doctrinaire and the theoretical. The problem before the Continental Congress is: How are they to help Boston? With noble declarations as to the rights of colonies? With fine words and expressions of sympathy? Or by a cessation of commerce with Britain, a weapon which has in the past proved effective?

"If it is to be such a cessation, every man in this room realizes that it cannot be purely voluntary, that we must have committees to watch and enforce. Shall we really refuse to take effective action because of theoretical considerations about the distribution of powers of government? Why, the Parliament which acts so unabashedly for the merchants of London would split their sides laughing at us."

To judge by the murmurs of agreement generated throughout the room, MacDougall was carrying a number of the merchants with him.

Jay resumed the exposition of his doubts with an impersonality which I found admirable.

"The fear of creating a new center of governmental power is not as doctrinaire as it might seem. A second center of allegiance would force the people to choose in their loyalties between the Continental Congress and the king. Given such terms, most would declare for the Congress. And that, I am afraid, might provide a tremendous instrument—a juggernaut, no less, which Sam Adams might seize upon and drive irresistibly straight down the broad highroad to his own aims."

MacDougall cut through the argument with an observation which had come into my own mind and which I felt I myself should have risen to present.

"The truly terrible thing would not be so much the

danger of a revolutionary surge as that the general populace would be given a hand in the management of affairs. Is that not so, Mr. Jay?"

"No and yes, Mr. MacDougall," Jay replied. "Believe me, I am not one of those who think we should be governed by a handful of the wealthiest. Yet I do mistrust the passions and judgment of the generality, and such mistrust is a factor in my thinking, quite as you point out."

At this, others of the Sons and of the merchants entered the discussion and the arguments began to go round and round in a general melee.

Finally, MacDougall again took the floor and addressed Jay. "Mr. Jay, suppose it turns out that the Congress does pass a resolution for nonintercourse and does call for committees of association to enforce it. Do you think New York should abide by such a decision?"

Again came hesitancy, genuine perplexity, and also candor.

"Perhaps the colonies would stand to lose more, and fatally so for the redress of their grievances, by disrupting their unanimity. I do not believe that at this juncture I would vote for the measure, yet if it were adopted I would recommend that New York continue to act in concert with the other colonies and abide by it."

"In that case," said MacDougall, "I suggest we need have no vote here deciding upon how to instruct Mr. Jay. I am content that we should give him free rein to exercise his judgment."

This met with a general outburst of approval.

As the gathering broke up I realized I felt greatly relieved that the discussion had been carried on mainly by Jay and MacDougall; it had not been necessary for me to express my own opinion. I had prided myself the past several days that while Kluger's ultimatum profoundly distressed me it had not in the least affected my actions. Yet here it was at work in a more subtle sense than I had imagined possible, beginning silently to constrain and to warp me.

13.

"OH, JAMIE, how I wish all these difficulties were over and we could devote ourselves more to each other."

"Believe me, I do, too."

Winter had come and gone, but my dilemma remained unresolved. During those long months, however, one thing had become clear to me: I could not and would not let go of Elisabeth. In one way or another she must remain part of my life.

We were seated on a bench at one side of the Common. Kluger had not flatly forbidden me to come visiting at his house, yet I felt more comfortable out from under his eyes.

As I looked across the sunny expanse of bright spring grass, islanded here and there with trees beneath which small groups enjoyed the Sabbath leisure, it seemed very difficult to believe that anything other than peace and serenity could reign here forever and ever.

Even as I gazed, however, I became aware of shouts and galloping hooves in one of the streets that led to the Common from the north. The hoofbeats stopped, then started up again, coming closer, then stopped once more. Again a clamor arose.

In another minute a rider spurred a foam-flecked horse out of Broadway right onto the grass near several groups of people. Excitedly he shouted at them. A number jumped up and shouted back. With a hurried reply he spurred his horse onward.

He galloped on along George's Street, where Elisabeth and I were sitting. I sprang from the bench and waved him down.

"What news?"

"Hear ye, hear ye," he shouted to the world at large, "the redcoats have attacked outside Boston and a great battle has been fought from Lexington to Concord. The redcoats have been whipped and driven all the way back to Boston and lie there now besieged by an army of minutemen. Great news! Great news! The redcoats have been whipped in a great battle fought all night long outside Boston!"

"Who sends you, fellow? I am a leader of the Sons, here. Show me credentials."

"Doctor Warren sends me," he replied in the same stentorian chant. "Here, see." He pulled a folded sheet of paper from a pocket. It bore the same news and was signed by Joseph Warren of the Boston Committee of Correspondence, and below his signature were signed the names of others in different towns on the route southward.

I threw him a salute. "When you want refreshment go to Hampden Hall."

He returned the salute and, putting spurs to his horse, galloped on.

"I cannot stay, my darling, not even to escort you back home," I said to Elisabeth.

I kissed her, and, at a run, started off across town to Alexander MacDougall's house.

As if the news were seeping out of the very sky onto all the town at once, north and south, east and west, drums began beating and fifes shrilling. People began to appear on the streets, seeking others with whom to verify the astounding event. Very soon, men carrying muskets began hurrying past, presumably to the assembly point of their militia unit.

MacDougall was pulling on his militia coat as I dashed into his house. "Is it true?" he boomed.

"Yes! I saw the dispatch rider's credentials."

"Get messages to the rest of the Sons committee! Tell them we're meeting in half an hour at the Hall!"

Sears and Willett were already on their way up the stairs as I came running down, and shortly we were all in the Sons committee room at Hampden Hall.

MacDougall opened the meeting by saying, "If we choose, we can act as though a war has begun. And I hope to God this committee will so choose! We can seize the various stores of the king's muskets, powder and shot, and really arm our waiting militia, and the people, too. We can smash the royal government by arresting the royal governor. And we can take over the port and put a stop to the flow of supplies to the British army at Boston."

Inside, I was vibrating to the many critical possibilities with which the day was pregnant, and to the all-at-once unknowable future. Were the others similarly affected? I wondered intensely. Some, such as MacDougall and Willett, appeared only to have expanded; they seemed to eat and drink the new atmosphere. It was as though they had known

121

all the time that it would come, and now that it was here, they were at home in it.

"If we do these things immediately and thoroughly," MacDougall continued, "before the king's troops in the harbor and at the fort can move to prevent us—or, better still, if in their small numbers they do move and we smash them utterly—there can thereafter be no turning back. We will have put it beyond the power of any faction in this city to paralyze the patriot cause further with temporizings and legalisms."

Not a man in the room saw it otherwise.

The cries and drummings outside the windows were growing in volume. We hastily defined the various tasks in the scheme and assigned them to the different committee members.

Lamb and Sears were to organize a great military parade through the town in order to raise the patriot indignation as high as possible and to concentrate its strength under the direction of the Sons. The clamor would serve, also, during a brief, vital interval, to lead the conservatives to think that clamor was all we intended.

Moving behind the fanfare, Willett was to arrest Acting Governor Colden. MacDougall was to take the Customs House with its records and its control of the wharves. And I was to seize the five hundred muskets stored in the City Hall and distribute them among the people.

Should we succeed, our committee would constitute the government, *de facto*, until a new governing body was created.

A bad mistake had been made by the conservatives when, out of their fear of the people, they had left them to the

Sons of Liberty to organize and drill. Our strength, at this crucial instant, lay in the fact that all the militia was ours.

The streets were now thronging with what seemed to be the entire populace. As I sped toward my lodgings I had to dodge crowds at every corner. Oddly enough, merrymakers, too, were out: shouters and brawlers and groups singing "Yankee Doodle," and spontaneous little parades that marched down the centers of streets chanting slogans, quite remarkably equipped, all at once and out of nowhere, with placards, bunting, and drums.

Perhaps a hundred of the Royal Irish Regiment were in barracks at the fort. And the sixty-four-gun ship of the line *Asia* had just come into the harbor several days before with we knew not how many additional troops. But I had as yet not caught a sign of any of these. Most of the British soldiers were at Boston.

I raced up the rear staircase of the inn to my room, flung off my Sunday clothes, and slipped into my militiaman's trousers and shirt. I had just slung on my bullet pouch and powder horn when in came Frank Rowe, Tommy's father, and my own foster father.

"Addie Simms was here about ten minutes ago, Jamie," he said. To Frank's usual solid, slow manner there was now added concern. "Very excited he was. Left a message. He's acting on emergency order number one—collecting the troops at the meeting point, where he will hold them for your arrival."

"At Peck's Slip?"

"Wouldn't say," Frank replied with a wry smile. "It's a secret. He said you'd know."

Elated, I slapped Frank on the arm. "We haven't lost a minute, then." I snatched my musket from the wall and made for the door. As I stepped out onto the open-air landing I turned. "Keep Tommy off the streets, Frank."

At the head of Peck's Slip I found more than eighty men of my unit, all armed and excited. I was almost overwhelmed by a sudden surge of emotion at the sight of so many who were so ready in the crisis.

"Addie, we've been given one of the most important tasks of the day," I said. "We're to capture the muskets in the City Hall."

"That's worth the drilling we've done!"

Addie was my lieutenant, quick and dependable, a fellow shipwright.

I turned to the men and called "Fall in!" And when I gave the command "Right face," a column of fours promptly came into existence.

The quickly growing crowd of onlookers clapped and cheered.

"Hooray for the patriot militia!" they shouted. "Hooray for Jamie Hardy and the liberties of America! Give us muskets, Jamie, and let us join in! We can shoot as well as Hillary Tanner there, or George Maurer. Come on, now, Jamie!"

"Fall in behind troops, those of you who will," I called, "and we'll see about muskets for you in a little while."

And off we marched into Water Street, everyone very much in step, our two drummers beating smartly, all of us showing what we had learned in our Sunday mornings of drilling.

With every minute, more joined us from the crowded,

cheering sidewalks and soon the tail of citizenry on the end of our column outnumbered the militia.

At Queen Street we had to halt to let a huge parade pass—none other than Sears' and Lamb's parade, with Sears at the head almost beside himself with grandiosity. He raised his musket wildly in salute, as though he were raising it to the heavens. The vast throng behind him was something to marvel at. Filling the street from walk to walk and almost four blocks long, the crowd must have numbered three or four thousand, all shouting and cheering.

When the great parade at last passed by we sped through the remaining streets at a run.

On arriving before the City Hall, I quickly drew the men out into a hollow, three-sided square which enclosed the front of the building. Then, with Addie and several others, I went up to the great double door and pounded on it.

No response came.

Addie and I examined the lock. "It can't be shot off," I said. "Axes are what we need."

"Axes!" Addie shouted back to the men.

"Axes!" The cry went up and down the street. In a few minutes half a dozen were being handed along through the crowd to us.

The massive doors were beautifully painted in gleaming white, and their elaborate scrollwork was meticulously done in gold, but there was no help for it. Two of the militiamen rapidly reduced one of the leaves to a mass of rent lumber.

Taking ten men with me, I passed through. And there behind the door cowered the caretaker, an old man, with one of his assistants.

"Quickly, now," I said, "the keys to the armory room."

"I—I cannot, sir," he faltered, obstinate enough in spite of his fear.

I hesitated. "Bring him along," I said. "Some of you go get a couple of axes."

We hurried on to the armory room, whose location in the north wing of the second floor I had long known. The door was locked, but a dozen raps smashed away its center panel. The long chamber within was immaculately clean. Neatly ranged along the walls and in files down the center were wooden cases, stacked almost ceiling high.

We pulled one down and with an axe I pried off the cover. Inside lay five new muskets, complete with rammers, all beautifully oiled. I rapidly counted one section and made an estimate of the entire room. Our five hundred muskets were here beyond doubt.

"Now," I said to Addie, "we'll move as swiftly as we can before the redcoats may arrive. Have the men find a table and a chair and set them out for me on the sidewalk—a second chair, too, come to think of it, and sit down Walter Thompson in it. Then start the men bringing the muskets out of here and onto the sidewalk beside the table. Perhaps they should pile up as many cases as possible in the entrance hall first, and rip the covers off the boxes there. When the muskets come out of the building I want them ready for distribution."

We went back to the street for a score more of men, and then, to make sure things went as I intended, I stayed and watched them carry out the first half dozen boxes. When I was satisfied, I left Addie in charge and went outside.

Beyond the cleared space held by the militiamen the street was filled with clamoring people to the end of the block in either direction. I would need no sentries other

126

than the crowd itself to let me know when the redcoats appeared.

On the sidewalk now stood a delicate little French-style table with thin, curved legs, all red and gold, and two ornamented chairs to match, their backs upholstered with red velvet. Beside the three bits of furniture lay the first cases of muskets. On one of the little chairs sat Walter Thompson, our clerk, a strapping carter, his board-covered portfolio open and his ink and pens waiting.

I came up to the table. "Walter, we're going to give out as many of these muskets as we can before the redcoats get here, and you're to make a list of those to whom I issue them."

Then I shouted to the crowd, "All able-bodied men who want to bear arms in the patriot cause, come forward! Form a line on this side, here, and the militiamen will let you pass through to the desk!"

A great cheer spread along the streets.

I sat down and scrutinized the first man to come through. He was short and stocky and excited-looking, but not frantic, in his bearing.

"Who are you, sir, and what do you do for a livelihood, and where do you live?"

"Harry Flint, if you will, and I am a joiner on Ann Street at the Sign of the Saw. I live there, at the sign."

"Who can vouch for you as a patriot and as a man?"

"By God, all who gather at the Cup and Roast on the corner of Ann and William—Henry de Cruik and Frank Allenby and Mel Stevens and others, too."

"Give him a musket," I said to the militiamen at the cases. "You have his name and address, Walter?"

Walter nodded, still writing.

The next in line was of medium height, thin and wiry, and near his middle years. Excitement danced in his eyes, too.

"Your name, sir, and calling, and where do you live?"

"Tim Arles, bless you, stonemason and tinsmith as well. I live on Prince Street at the Sign of the Black Cloud, and I have lived there these thirty-nine years, since I was born, in truth. I am well known there and only last week I mended the spits at your own stepfather's Spread Sail Inn, Master Jamie Hardy."

"A musket," I said.

The next in line was tall and shambling, with a grin that went up only one side of his face and with something overly friendly about him.

"Your name, sir, and calling, and where do you live?"

He stopped short and his great friendliness dropped away. He stared at Walter, who waited with his pen in the air, and then suddenly indignant—too indignant—he shouted, "Is it a list of names you're making so the redcoats will have no trouble knowing whom to come and hang! You should be handing out muskets, not making up lists of names!"

"No musket," I said. "Next man."

But he stepped forward boldly and stooped quickly over the case to seize a musket for himself. I half rose and buffeted him across the chest so that he staggered. The quick hands of the militiamen were upon him at once and he was outside the square again.

The next man was tipsy.

"No musket."

And the next man had something sly about him that made

128

me loath to arm him, although he was ready enough with his replies.

"No musket," I said.

When we had given out some two hundred weapons, a militiaman ran in with a note from MacDougall.

"Collector of the Port refuses to give up keys to Customs House and I am going to assault it. Think I can carry the building with the men I have now, but want to make certain. Can you lend me any men of yours?"

I now had a hundred and fifty militiamen and, in addition, there remained with us most of those to whom we had given muskets.

"Have you heard or seen anything of the redcoats?" I asked the courier.

"Not a sign. We think they're being held in barracks till reinforcements can be brought in off the *Asia*."

I decided to risk sending MacDougall a large detachment, reasoning that the greater his force the sooner the Customs House would be taken and my men returned to me. I sent him off fifty of my regulars and fifty of those to whom we had just given weapons.

Before an hour was out they were all back, jubilant. When the Port Collector had seen the Sons close in with arms at the ready he had hung out a flag of white handkerchiefs. MacDougall controlled the Customs House —keys, records, stamps, building, and all—and no ship could clear the harbor without the sanction of the Sons. There would be no more provisioning of the British troops at Boston from New York.

I now sent out men from each end of the street to see what could be discovered about the redcoats. They returned in a little while with the news that none had been seen or heard of. But Acting Governor Colden, they learned, had escaped us. He had gotten wind of the Sons' intention to seize him and had managed to flee across the East River to Long Island.

A messenger arrived from Marinus Willett. He had captured the powder house on Freshwater Pond and did I need any powder or did I want any other help? I sent the messenger back with thanks, congratulating Willett and saying I needed no aid.

Save for the loss of the governor our plans were being fulfilled. Soon, even if the British should land a large force from the *Asia*, we would be able to unite our groups and overwhelm them.

When we had given out almost three hundred muskets I decided that two hundred should be retained as a reserve. They would go well with Willett's captures from the powder house.

I sent a messenger off to MacDougall asking his opinion on this.

In about twenty minutes the messenger returned. At the Customs House he had been directed to seek MacDougall at Rodman's Slip, where he had found him in most serious conference with Lamb. MacDougall had discovered from the Customs House records that there were two ships tied up there loaded with supplies for the British troops at Boston and ready to go out on the next tide.

MacDougall thought it an excellent idea to hold two hundred of the muskets; and when I was able, he wished me to come to Rodman's Slip with as many of my men as possible. He intended to board the two vessels, whose masters were defying him. The tide would not be favorable for them until seven o'clock.

"We'll now remove the remaining muskets to Hampden Hall," I announced. "After that we have a difficult task to perform. It will engage us till late in the evening, but I trust there will be no defections on this account."

Cheerful shouts came from all about.

I sent off squads to discover carts and dray horses, and all bent to the work. Case followed case down from the armory room and out the smashed front door. At last four wagons stood in a row, ready, each bearing ten neatly stacked wooden containers.

Quite according to the manuals, we organized a convoy with a strong rear guard and outriders, and we moved out and off to Hampden Hall.

The excited throngs in the streets had not abated a whit. If anything, there were more people out now than earlier. They cheered us all along the route, and joked:

"Are you fellows carrying coffins for the ministry?"

"Where are you going to bury the governor?"

When we arrived at the Hall I pressed for dispatch in transferring the muskets to the cellar. The forthcoming assault on the ships weighed upon me, as it was now close to five o'clock.

Half an hour was consumed unloading the wagons. Then I addressed the company in the street before the Hall. "Our next task is to assist the forces under Mr. MacDougall and Mr. Lamb in detaining two ships that are now at Rodman's Slip. Unless we prevent it, they'll sail on the seven o'clock tide with provisions for the redcoats in Boston. Is there anyone who would rather go home to his supper than help strike this next blow?"

"No, no, no," came with much laughter. "Come on, Jamie, let's get down to the wharves."

We made a column of fours again and quick-marched to the river.

During the swift passage I turned over in my mind two striking manifestations of the popular temper. Though the day was waning, the excitement among the people was not at all subsiding. To the contrary, there was a groundswell of the general detestation of England, of a strength even I had not fully comprehended.

And, again, in addressing the men about the ships, there had been a note of challenge in my voice, for I had assumed that some would have to be taunted into remaining. But they had all, to a man, only laughed, and not one had gone off.

If the feelings of the men in the other colonies were as deep and powerful, then on this very day a new nation was emerging upon the earth. Whatever might follow—the fighting, perhaps, and the ceremonial trappings—would be later, outward manifestations of the great will and spirit crystalizing today.

Now we were running down broad, cobblestoned Water Street, the wharves on our left stretching vast and black into the sunless river.

In Rodman's Slip two great ships reared their bows high above the pavement. Across the street waited several files of militiamen, who cheered good-humoredly as we approached.

On the river side of the street, beneath the bowsprits, stood a knot of men with angry, set faces. Among them I saw MacDougall and Lamb. "You've done well, Jamie!"

MacDougall exclaimed as I joined them. He turned back to those in the group who were strangers to me. "So far as I am concerned, gentlemen, our discussions are at an end. I will only repeat to you our determination that not an ounce of flour or gunpowder will clear this port for the British at Boston."

"Sail we shall," came the retort. The speaker was apparently the master of one of the ships and his tone was that of one accustomed to command.

He turned, now, along with the others, and strode back to his ship.

"I'd hoped to intimidate them by a show of numbers alone," said MacDougall. "Now, let's lose no time. Jamie, divide your men between Kendricks' and Wilson's units, and one group to a ship, we'll board. We already have grappling hooks and ladders. Tell the men not to shoot first but to make a good display of their muskets. I don't think the seamen are so ready to lay down their lives for the delivery of the provisions as are the masters."

As it turned out, MacDougall had estimated the attitudes of the crews correctly. When we rushed the ships we discovered the sailors had neglected even to draw up their ladders. None defended the bulwarks.

I came over the side in the group led by Sears, who was himself foremost up the ladder, and as he, Kendricks, myself, and three or four others jumped to the deck, leveling our muskets, only the master and one of the mates met us, pistols in hand. The few others visible behind masts and hatches were there clearly against their will.

As our militiamen poured over the bulwarks, it became obvious that the shipmaster's defiance was futile. Sears roared an order, and he and his mate dropped their pistols. When they were safely under guard in the cabin, we filled the ship with our own men and set about unloading her.

What we lacked in experience we made up in zest. We lit all the lamps we could find against the oncoming dusk. Working whatever windlasses we could, and manhandling a great deal more of the cargo up from the holds, we kept it moving back out onto the wharf. In about two hours we had both ships emptied.

The moon was rising and it was near half past eight as we picked our way amidst the spread-out cargo, ticking off flour and canvas and gunpowder and other such desirable items, which were to be stored for the future by the Sons. The perishable foodstuffs we would sell the next day at auction and the proceeds would be forwarded to Boston.

By eleven o'clock we had removed what we wanted to cellars and warehouses. Guards were posted over the remainder of the cargos, and, for relief, commands were given over to others.

The long day was at an end.

14.

FOR ALMOST A WEEK the patriot militia controlled the city.

We marched the streets exuberantly, brawling a bit out of an excess of spirits and tarring and feathering some of the more foolishly arrogant Tories, but, in the main, displaying the determination with which we meant to keep the city for the patriot cause.

In a few days, however, it became clear that a government of some sort was needed to replace the royal government we had shattered.

Five days after the great Sunday of revolt the different factions in the city came together at the home of James Duane. Under blazing chandeliers, behind window blinds that were drawn tightly so as not to draw fire from the two British warships in the harbor, we debated the situation.

Alexander MacDougall spoke for the Sons: "There is no real difficulty here. At the time the Continental Congress adopted the Association in order to enforce nonintercourse we set up a committee to oversee its operation in this colony. We can expand this committee to, say, one hundred and, by giving it our allegiance, endow it with general powers to govern."

From the conservative side of the room came silence.

Kluger, seated at right angles to me so that his strong, flat-nosed profile showed sharply, said finally, "It seems a most cavalier way to treat so important a thing as government—to cast off one because of a disturbance in the streets, and to create another simply by adding more people to a committee."

Another silence followed. All sensed that the real issue was nowhere near being touched upon.

Marinus Willett, as though to keep himself amused during the general evasion by pursuing this extraneous thought, said, "I think you will find that every government presently ruling on this earth traces its origin to some act of disturbance—either in the streets or on the battlefield. What really makes a government acceptable is whether it suits the needs of those it governs, and whether it has their support. I trust I am not being pedantic."

Kluger and the other merchants glared at him.

In effect, the Sons and their militia had enfranchised themselves, and it was our own committee that now ruled the city, even if temporarily. And we did not mean for the merchants to take the franchise away again.

Then John Jay's voice rose, seeming hesitant, but really firm enough, as I was learning.

"Such a new committee as Mr. MacDougall suggests would, of course, require the sanction of the body politic, and to achieve this we must call for an election and have the committee duly approved." His words went to the heart of the issue the merchants wished to avoid—the matter of franchise.

Kluger stared at Jay with vexation, his face mirroring what was passing in the minds of the other merchants: elections now, with the adherents of the Sons marching the streets and flourishing muskets, would be elections in which all would have the right to vote. At this juncture no man could be denied the suffrage on the grounds that he lacked the forty pounds' property qualification. And once established, the franchise would be accepted as permanent.

"What think you of Mr. Jay's proposal, Jamie?" exclaimed MacDougall expansively, almost jovially.

I started guiltily, as though I were being called to account for not having spoken up earlier.

The entire room turned to me for the moment, but I saw only Kluger—grim, already exasperated at Jay's comment, his eyes small and bright and hard.

"Why, I say that of course there must be an election—to give the new government the only kind of mandate any government can rightfully have: acceptance by the people it governs. And equally important, it must be a truly democratic election. Every grown man must cast a vote, whether he be a drayman or a great and wealthy merchant."

Kluger continued to stare at me, still grim, and now impassive. It seemed to me his eyes were even smaller and harder.

John Jay spoke again. "Why, yes, I do not see how it is possible, at the moment, to deny the mass of the citizenry the right to participate in choosing the new government."

Kluger turned on Jay in concert with all the other merchants.

"But Mr. Jay!" exclaimed Daniel Robbins, the silk importer. "We are in the midst of these difficulties, after all, because we feel our property is being taken away by a dangerously unrestrained British government. This new viewpoint of yours puts us in peril of having it taken away by the furious rabble right here at home. The poor are of course in the majority and will outvote us on all issues. Do you not fear utter anarchy?"

Jay replied, "With respect to anarchy, we stand in greater danger of it this very moment if we refuse to make the compromise of a democratic suffrage. This morning, for example, Mr. Washburton of John Street, a Tory, true enough, was so incautious as to vent his spleen in remarks he shouted from the upper floor of his home at a passing band of the militia. They did not hesitate to enter his house, drag him out into the street, strip him to the waist, and pour hot tar and a pillowful of feathers upon him. This morning, too, the entire cargo of the *Excelsior* was taken out of the ship on the mere rumor she carried provisions intended for the British at Boston, and was sold up at auction then and there on the wharf. These are now daily occurrences. And the various bands of the general mob hesitate less and less to act on the merest suspicion.

"Would you have even the greater questions of policy, such as our relations with Great Britain and what is to be done about the imminent arrival of Governor Tryon decided by the same unruly mob?

"The second consideration is that here and now we may all collaborate in choosing the slate of committee members which will be presented to the electorate. And in return for the compromise we of the propertied elements make in admitting the general citizenry to the vote, the Sons of Liberty will surely accept candidates for the committee who may not in all cases be to their liking."

Jay paused to glance questioningly at MacDougall. Mac-Dougall gravely nodded.

"So, gentlemen, I suggest that those of us who are of what might be called the more conservative attitude spend as little time as is needful in absorbing the fact that a popular suffrage has become the reality. Let us proceed to the choosing of a slate."

Where Jay led, the merchants were beginning to follow. The franchise question was soon considered settled. And then began the horse trading between the factions concerning who should sit on the new committee—the Committee of One Hundred.

I cast a glance every so often at Kluger. He looked by turns angry, bemused, as though possibly absorbing the forward march of events, but with difficulty, and, very infrequently, interested in the arguments. His eyes rested for the most part on Jay. And whenever he happened to glance in my general direction he looked through and beyond me as though he were examining an open window.

"And there's something else. I've been nominated to the new Committee of One Hundred. In a week, if the people pass favorably on our recommendations, I'll be one of those who rule the city."

This was the news that had prompted me to risk insult from Kluger by coming at once to visit Elisabeth at her home. I knew it would delight her.

"Oh, Jamie, Jamie," she exclaimed, hugging me. "It's only the first step. You'll be mayor of the city some day and a governor of the province!"

"How could anyone doubt it," I said, laughing, and

accepting a kiss as my reward. "Or even the head of a free and independent union of all the colonies. You know, the committee that ruled before this one created a colony-wide Provincial Congress, a legislature to replace the Tory-Loyalist one. Now that this congress is sitting, despite all its conservatives, New York will take its place among the other colonies moving forward—possibly to independence."

Elisabeth smiled, but her voice was sober. "Must it come to that?" she asked. "With an army on our side and governments in most of the colonies that are favorable to the patriot cause, perhaps we can bargain now for the kind of settlement we want, and there need be no more fighting."

"The English milords don't intend to bargain. You mark my words. Every place outside England is another Ireland or India to them. It's independence and liberty for us, or else slavery. And after we've established an independent nation, my sweet, you and I will live in a little cottage in Greenwich Village and have four children—two boys and two girls—and if your father votes to my liking on the forthcoming Committee of One Hundred I shall be gracious enough in return to consent to having one of my sons named after him!"

"How very accommodating of you," came the heavy, ironic tones of Kluger himself from the doorway, where he stood all at once in hat and cloak.

I nearly dropped the glass of sherry I had just raised toward the ceiling in a toast to the future.

"Yes, sir," I said more softly. "I shall even name one of my daughters after your late wife."

"Provided I vote correctly, of course, on the Committee of One Hundred."

140

"I'm not by nature tyrannical, sir," I replied. "I can brook differences of opinion, to a degree."

"Such good fortune is almost more than I deserve," he responded. "On June twenty-fifth Governor Tryon is to land, returning from England. How do you think I ought to vote on the question of what attitude the committee should adopt toward him?"

"We ought to pitch him into the harbor, sir," I said, my tone deferential.

"Even though he will arrive with a man-of-war, which will make three in the harbor by then—three warships that could raze this town to the ground in six or seven hours?"

"Oh, come, Papa," exclaimed Elisabeth, "this isn't your new Committee of One Hundred. Shall I pour you some sherry?"

"Yes, do," said Kluger. "It was a long meeting. For the life of me I don't see how you got down here so quickly, Hardy."

"It's the incentive, sir. And I warn you that just as soon as possible I shall become your son-in-law."

"That's a warning not to be taken lightly," he said, removing his cloak and hat and seating himself. His tone was not by any means humorous. He was still angry over the way things had gone at the meeting. It might well take him weeks to get over Jay's change of attitude, and after that, months, if ever, really to accept the outrageous perils of a democratic suffrage.

"Thank you, my dear," he said to Elisabeth after she gave him a glass. He watched her set down the decanter and then drop onto the sofa beside me.

He drank the entire glassful at one draught. "Now that

the Continental Congress has decided it must have an army and has appointed a commander-in-chief, I suppose it will be nothing less than treason for me to greet Tryon courteously and decently—our governor though he still is." His voice was again heavy with sarcasm, and even bitterness.

Deferentially, I said, "On the very same day that Tryon is expected to arrive, General Washington will also arrive in this city on his way to Boston to take up the command there of the Continental Congress' army. It is the oddest of coincidences, but fact, nevertheless. If I greet him as our commander-in-chief, will you consider me a rebel to the Crown?"

Kluger gnawed his lower lip and stared.

"What I don't want," he burst out, "is a handful of wild New England farmers declaring war for me against the greatest maritime power on earth. It doesn't make sense. And I don't want to compound their idiocy by declaring war here in New York. To kick Tryon out will be to endorse just such a declaration of war."

"You're on the committee to greet General Washington. Is that what you intend to tell him?"

"By God, yes! And to make sure he doesn't fail to understand!"

"Even after the events at Boston, and of last Sunday, here?"

"All that happened last Sunday here was that a small group of irresponsibles got out of hand."

With this he caught me on the raw. Barely containing my anger, I decided it was time to take my leave.

"The hour is late," I said. I raised Elisabeth's fingers to my lips. "Good night. And good night, sir, to you."

15.

THE SPRING was ripening into a glorious summer. Along the vast valley of the Hudson all lay crystal clear under the bright, hot sun. The great oaks and elms were heavy with foliage; and between the undulating hills on this side and the red cliffs of the Palisades on the other there shimmered the broad, dazzling, wind-and-current-torn surface of the river.

Behind me, along the huge natural lawns that softened the high bank, armed men waited, deployed in military formations. I turned my eyes from them back to the dot which had separated itself from the Hoboken shore some time before and now grew slowly. Much was coming to mind while we waited for the ferryboat to make its transit of the river.

Perhaps a hundred yards or so along the bank southward of me stood the Lispenard mansion, and before its portico waited Kluger in company with a group of merchants. Later on this very day he would stand attendance upon Governor Tryon when that worthy stepped ashore at the Battery.

I walked along the front of my company. At the end of

143

the formation I gazed rearward toward the highway. There, in a wide glade, stood a semicircle of carriages from which the occupants, like the soldiers and the thousands of townspeople ranged all around, looked riverward, watching the approach of the broad-hulled ferryboat.

The Kluger carriage was among them and in it sat Elisabeth, back straight and face aglow. I waved till I caught her eye, and when she saw me she waved her handkerchief excitedly in return.

The great barge was coming close now, its oars individually distinct as they rose and fell. Along with everyone else I tried to pick out the man who had been appointed supreme commander for the military forces of all the colonies. But there were too many on the barge, and the uniforms were too varied for me to make any meaning out of the groupings.

Soon, the militiamen stationed at the water's edge were wading out into the river to seize the cast lines, while the oarsmen dug in to hold the barge steady. One by one the figures aboard came ashore, and then, all at once, there was no doubt. He stood head and shoulders above the others, and as he sprang to land, those who had preceded him turned to wait upon his next movements.

Our welcoming committee approached. Military salutes were exchanged, an animated conversation took place, and then the two groups began the climb up the bank by way of a nearby path.

From one company commander after another came the long-drawn-out wail ordering the waiting formations to attention. The commander-in-chief would review the troops on his way to the Lispenard mansion.

A second series of commands arose, starting at the end of

144

the line nearest the pathway, and soon all nine companies stood presenting arms.

And then, there he was, very tall, rawboned, dressed in a blue uniform with a white plume in his hat, and striding along the uneven ground quickly and steadily, his large, square-jawed face turned to the troops, seriously observing of us what he could.

Then he was outside my field of vision and passing before the next company.

When the last company had been reviewed and set at ease we began to cheer, soldiers and citizenry alike. The tall figure, now quite distant, raised his plumed hat in acknowledgment and disappeared into the Lispenard mansion.

Two more barges put in, bearing the commander's escort, a detachment of light horse from Philadelphia, and we busied ourselves helping the newcomers.

But I acted with only a part of my mind. I was preoccupied with thoughts about the commander. This man would certainly have an enormous influence on our policy. Was he, I wondered, one of those who felt no war was going on—even now, after the news of the battle of Bunker Hill—that the colonies were still merely taking precautionary measures? Was he, perhaps, another of those Southern Sultans who reigned on their plantations, slavers interested solely in rescuing themselves from their debts to their London factors? Or did he see himself as the leader of military forces that were engaged in a revolution?

"Major Hardy! Major Hardy!" someone called.

"Here, lad, what's the matter?"

"You're wanted at the Lispenards'."

"In there?"

"Right away, sir, if you please."

I turned to Addie Simms, who raised his eyebrows at me. With a nod I gave Addie the command and hurried off after the messenger.

In a large chamber on the ground floor I found those who had just debarked from the ferryboat gathered together with our welcoming committee and various later arrivals. New uniforms abounded, of many designs and colors, and it struck me how, for the first time, they overwhelmed the darker hues of civilian dress.

The general was seated in a chair placed between two tall windows. His long legs were crossed, yet he seemed not at all to be lounging but to sit easily erect.

Alexander MacDougall, wearing his new blue general's uniform, stepped forward and took me by the arm. He led me up to General Washington and said, "This is Major Hardy. He is the person best acquainted with the details of our powder supply."

I saluted, and the general saluted swiftly and soberly in return. His eyes were large, gray, and unhurriedly observant.

"I am pleased to make your acquaintance, Major," he said in a voice that was pleasantly resonant. "We have just received a dispatch from the troops at Boston giving further information on the new battle that has been fought there, at Bunker Hill. It appears that our own side had to retire from its positions, at the last, mainly because of the general paucity of powder. And this causes me the gravest concern. It is about the supplies of powder available elsewhere in the colonies that I now seek information. Can you tell me with some precision how much is to be had in your city at this moment?"

146

The courteous, warm voice betrayed a considerateness that was in curious contrast with the uncompromising eyes.

"Up to yesterday we had one thousand and four barrels of powder, sir," I replied. "Today we have only four barrels. Yesterday we sent one thousand barrels to Boston."

He studied me in silence. Then, in a lower tone, he said, "Thank you, Major. You bring me good news on the matter of my chiefest worry."

There was an awkward interval as I wondered whether I should salute and leave. But the general himself gave no sign that the interview was ended. Though there was no change in his expression and he continued to look at me, he seemed to be communing with himself.

At last he spoke again. "This is my first journey about the colonies in many a year, Major," he said, quite as though he were explaining himself to some superior body such as a committee of the Continental Congress. "As you may understand, I should like to acquaint myself, as well as the hasty circumstances permit, with the temper of the people. You saluted well. And the troops outside stood their formation excellently. Yet you appear too young, all of you, to have had professional experience. Tell me how you've managed this."

"Like everyone else in our nine companies, sir," I replied, "I have hunted these surrounding woods since my childhood, so that usage of firearms is second nature to me. The military arts we have studied out of British army manuals. We have been training ourselves this past year or more. And, also, we count among us a few veterans of previous wars, such as General MacDougall, here, who guide and correct us."

The general nodded, once, slowly. "I must go on to other

147

matters, now, Major Hardy, but I hope that we will someday meet again."

I saluted, he returned the salute, and I faced about and left.

I found my way outside and walked back to my company in a daze of competing emotions. The strongest among them seemed to be admiration, or perhaps awe, and best of all, great relief at an instinctive realization that we had truly found a military commander.

We formed a great parade to escort General Washington into town, and when he seated himself in the open carriage, we moved off down the Greenwich road, the mightiest spectacle in the city's memory.

First came the nine companies of militia—over a thousand men, muskets all pointing skyward at the same angle, and all stepping briskly to the beat of the drums. Then came the members of the Provincial Congress, a sober group whose walk now contrasted curiously with the march-step of the soldiery and whose broadcloth appeared suddenly drab against the colorful uniforms.

After these came the general's retinue: subordinate commanders and adjutants, all in uniform, most quite young, their expressions mirroring a mixture of pride, determination, uncertainty as to their place, and responsibility. I understood, for I felt the same when in formation.

Behind these came the general himself, his carriage drawn by two white horses. He sat alone on the rear seat, and on the seat facing him sat two other patriot commanders who were, I learned, generals Lee and Schuyler. He neither smiled nor waved but took his part with gravity in this demonstration of solidarity against the British.

Behind him, on glistening horses, cantered a long double file of the Philadelphia Light Horse in bright blue coats with scarlet facings and yellow breeches. And following upon all these came the townsfolk, a great winding column numbering perhaps five thousand, cheering in holiday mood.

For such a glorious display it endured all too briefly. The parade had scarcely stretched itself full length upon the highway when the mile or so to town was traversed and we were standing in the streets of the city outside Hull's, where the general was to spend the night.

A hubbub arose beside the general's carriage when a group of petitioners sought access to him. It turned out that these were none other than a committee from the Provincial Congress, and the general gave his consent.

He climbed lithely from the vehicle and took up a stand on the sidewalk while his entourage ranged itself about him.

None other than Isaac Low, among the most conservative of our merchants, now stepped forward and made a deep bow. He unfolded a sheet of paper and announced that the sentiments he was about to express embodied the hopes of the Provincial Congress of the Colony of New York.

The speech he delivered was brief enough, but its unctuously rounded phrases expressed admonitions and injunctions of a tenor that seemed to me disgraceful.

"While we deplore the calamities of this divided Empire," the address began, "we rejoice in the appointment of a gentleman from whose abilities and virtues we are taught to expect both security and peace."

And then, repeating to General Washington that his duty lay in the maintenance of peace, it went on to instruct him:

"We have the most flattering hopes of success in the glorious struggle for American liberty and the fullest assurance that whenever this important contest shall be decided by that fondest wish of each American soul, an accommodation with the mother country, you will cheerfully resign the important deposit committed into your hands and reassume the character of our worthiest citizen."

Eyebrows rose amongst those surrounding the general. This was an odd way to encourage a newly appointed commander—to tell him to seek an "accommodation" and then to suggest he look about for the first opportunity to resign.

But the general himself did not flicker an eyelash. Without so much as clearing his throat, and speaking in the same forthright tone I had heard him use from his chair, only now raised with ease to encompass the entire street, he said, "Gentlemen, at the same time as with you I deplore the necessity of such an appointment as that with which I am now honored, be assured that every exertion of my worthy colleagues and myself will be equally extended to the reestablishment of peace and harmony with the mother country, as to the fatal but necessary operations of war."

And then he concluded with a sentence whose ring has never left my memory: "When we assumed the soldier we did not lay aside the citizen, and we shall most sincerely rejoice with you in that happy hour when the establishment of American liberty upon the most firm and solid foundations should enable us to return to our private stations in the bosom of a free, peaceful, and happy country."

An entire code of principles stood here for the moment revealed. I wondered excitedly whether he had read and pondered Locke and Rousseau and Beccaria even as I had.

It seemed to me for an instant that, Southern Sultan and all, he was one of us—almost one of the Sons!

With a courtly bow he signified that his reply was at an end. The committee, chagrin hidden behind tight-lipped faces, returned the bow, and the general entered Hull's.

16.

MACDOUGALL AND I watched the dismissed militia leave and the crowds disperse. Then, rapidly, we walked southward.

Sure enough, at the Battery, between the Exchange and the river, waited another committee. We were almost late. A boat crowded with uniformed figures was already approaching from the latest royal ship in the harbor.

This committee, too, had been appointed by the Provincial Congress. And the disgraceful and exasperating truth was that it contained some of the very same people who had been on hand to receive the general. Kluger stood here, bearing the same concerned expression he had worn at the Lispenard mansion while awaiting the appearance of the patriot commander-in-chief.

The question as to which of the two arrivals should be greeted officially by the Provincial Congress had been the first important business to face the newly assembled colony-wide legislature. To the exasperation of those of us like myself, who sat for the Sons, we found ourselves again in a minority. The conservatives of the city had joined with the conservatives and out-and-out Tories of the upstate regions to evade the issue with an incredible compromise: committees would be sent to welcome both the leader of the revolutionary army and the returning royal governor.

No parade of determined militia or enthusiastic citizenry accompanied this committee. And the thin crowd here bore the aspect of curious onlookers who would enjoy any kind of a spectacle.

On hand in plenty were worthies of the old sort. There was the governor's doughty council, faces scarcely seen on the streets for two years past, and some from the old Assembly, of which so little had been heard since the tea dumping. All were primped out in their finest lace. Their buckles and chains and walking sticks glinted and glittered bravely. And making shameful fraternity with these were no less than a dozen elected members of the supposedly patriot Provincial Congress.

To add to the irony, a company of our own militia patrolled the water's edge, on guard against any attempt to land troops from the warships to seize General Washington.

Just as the water was turning gray-black with the declining sun, the governor's boat made fast in Whitehall Slip. Up the ferry stairs came the estimable William Tryon himself, absent in England these two years for the treatment of an ailment, and never for one moment missed during that period by the great bulk of the people.

He wore a heavily brocaded scarlet coat and yellow breeches, a hat glittering with gold lace sufficient for a dozen admirals, and an expression of habitual, ill-natured imperiousness—the last tempered somewhat for the moment, no doubt, by information that the armed patriot militia officered by the Sons of Liberty was in undisputed control of the city.

Still, his pouchy, hawklike face was so overbearing in its demeanor that had the nearby militiamen been of my own company, I would have ordered his arrest then and there for the sheer pleasure of publicly humiliating him.

He marched across the cobbled street from the slip to the Exchange accompanied by some dozen red-coated aides, and was at once ceremoniously and devotedly engaged by the crowd of waiting functionaries. All bowed deeply, and as Tryon briskly replied in kind they all bowed again.

Benjamin Kissam now stepped forth and delivered himself of expressions of welcome not audible to the onlookers. Whatever his message, he himself was so moved that at the end of his recital he swept the ground again with his hat in another deep genuflection.

Tryon once more responded quickly, and even with some annoyance. It occurred to me he was nervous at his present situation, as well he might be with the militiamen watching him hostilely from the shore.

He uttered several curt sentences which he did not bother to accompany with a smile, and as several hoots mingled with the scattered huzzahs, he stepped forward, moving his procession on its way. The entire group that landed with him now proceeded down Broad Street to the house of Hugh Wallace, where the governor was apparently to stay.

I watched with indignation as the arrogant little knot of men moved on to take up its accustomed positions, and rule as of old. For an angry and baffled moment it seemed to me that all we had striven for and gained was now nullified. Here, once more, and despite everything, we had a royal governor amongst us.

Within the hour the Sons committee gathered at Hampden Hall.

"Imagine the pompous, strutting fool parading our streets like any English lord in his shire! Just as though Lexington and Bunker Hill had never taken place! And that sniveling, crawling, toadying crew of so-called patriots making up to him, each and every one of them still yearning for a baronetcy!"

So stormed Sears.

Marinus Willett pursed his lips and nodded before adding, "The colonies north and south are engaged in a war and we in New York are busy returning to the Crown its privileges and prerogatives!"

"Let's arrest the beggar here and now!" shouted Sears. "To the devil with the Provincial Congress and that whole crew! I'll take a militia company and show him how much of a governor he is. I'll halt him on every street corner and tweak his nose there for the benefit of all!"

"Arrest him we ought," said MacDougall. "That way we'll get round the lickspittle Provincial Congress."

But he spoke carefully, weighing his thoughts and words, and something in his manner roused Sears' impatience.

"Well, then, why delay?" he snapped.

"Suppose they open up on the town with their ships' guns. Naval guns would do us a great deal of damage."

"I doubt they'll bombard," said Willett.

At this I swung my attention about sharply. "Why wouldn't they?" I asked.

"Because New York is the best barracks town for them in all North America. It is at the center of the colonies, it is a great port, and, God forgive us, this province is the most sympathetic to them. They would hope to save it and take it

155

entire, most especially if they have to sail out of their present entrapment at Boston."

We argued the probabilities.

"I have a way to probe their intentions beforehand," said MacDougall.

The general wrangling ceased.

"Let's first make a military strike in the town—one that will profit us regardless of what happens thereafter—and see how they react to it. I have such a move in mind."

We continued to listen.

"I suggest we seize the cannon that ring the Battery and command the harbor. As of this moment there are still only a handful of British troops among us here on land and it will be easy to do. Once the cannon are ours any struggle with the ships that may follow will be so much easier for us."

We saw the point.

"When?"

"This very night. And tomorrow it will be Tryon's turn."

The same night two of our companies made their way in small detachments as quietly as possible through the silent streets. One company was commanded by MacDougall and one by myself. We carried ladders, ropes, and levers in addition to our arms, and we trundled along with us small carts, cursing a bit at the continual low thunder made by the iron-rimmed cart wheels against the cobbles.

We arrived at the high, broad battery wall that dominated the bay without arousing a single British soldier in the adjacent fort. And without drawing attention from the ships, or so we thought.

Swiftly, we raised the ladders, climbed atop the wall

156

bearing levers and pickaxes, and fell to work prying the guns out of their mountings.

For half an hour everything went smoothly. One by one the guns came loose and we lowered them to the carts. It was almost as though the redcoats in the fort had elected not to hear all our pounding and screeching; which was easy enough to believe, as there were very few of them, used lately for ceremonial only, and without stomach for real fighting as we had found out in various scuffles even before we had organized our militia.

We were beginning to congratulate ourselves on our success when from the water side of the wall came the clatter and squealing of oarlocks. Into the dim light cast by our shaded lamps hove a boat filled with redcoats. It could have been an ordinary patrol or it could have been a special mission sent out to investigate the noise on the wall.

MacDougall ordered more militiamen with weapons to mount the wall. Those at work on the remaining cannon redoubled their efforts.

It seemed to me that the boat, crowded as it was, constituted more than a routine patrol. The distance, in the night, was barely too great to read expressions on faces, but not to catch the faint glint of readied weapons.

All at once a musket flared in the boat. The shot resounded. For an astonished moment silence hung in the night air. Then, from along the wall, muskets exploded in response and white jets of water spurted up around the boat. Perhaps bullets landed inside it as well, but we heard no cries.

Tensely, we watched the oars churn and bite the water in wild, short chops to back her off. The redcoats did not fire again, and we let them pull out of the light and off toward the *Asia* without sending additional bullets after them.

We turned back to the cannon. The last of the heavy brass nine-pounders was finally lifted down. We had stripped the wall completely of its twenty-one pieces of ordnance.

Our caravan had barely begun the journey to the Common when we heard a burst of cannon fire. Cannonballs moaned above us and crashed all around, smashing into houses and thundering along streets. The guns of the *Asia* were firing. Spurts of flame appeared at the muzzles as, with deep-throated barks, they launched their projectiles.

Windowpanes shattered. Odd-looking holes appeared instantaneously in gables, showing the dark blue sky and the stars on the other side. Planks and tiles and tree branches sailed about and clattered into the street.

In another minute the bombardment ceased. People with coats thrown over nightclothes came running out of their houses, some to rush back in again, and all in a state of confusion.

The silence of the guns continued, and I was sure that the cannonade was over. I felt an odd exhilaration, which stayed with me as we dragged the captured cannon to the Liberty Pole beside the Common, arranged them in concentric semicircles, and mounted a proper guard over them.

As soon as this was done I hurried back downtown to the Bowling Green and the Kluger house.

A glance told me no damage had been done here. The large, many-gabled house reposed its dark bulk in silence under the starry sky.

I turned my steps back uptown, staring with fascination as I went at the shattered glass and ripped planks lying here

158

and there along the streets, and the fresh, white wounds on the tree trunks.

I had scarcely laid my head on the pillow, it seemed to me, when there came a rapping at my door that paused and started up again, paused and started up, but would not cease.

When I finally rose to open I saw by the sunlight that the morning was full blown.

On the landing outside stood Benjamin, Kluger's coachman.

"Mr. Kluger wishes you to come at once, sir."

"At once?"

"He wishes to discuss something with you that is extremely urgent—the most urgent matter you and he could discuss. He made me repeat this over until he felt sure I had it correctly."

"Very well."

"I have the carriage with me."

"Whew! As soon as I wash, Benjamin."

"An additional word, sir, in confidence. He is most angry. I have never before seen him in such a passion."

Some twenty minutes later I was being led into the sitting room at the Kluger house, where, all alone, Kluger waited, scarce able to contain himself till the door had fairly closed on Benjamin.

"Damn! Damn! Damn! Hardy," he exploded. "You and that gang of wild men have done it this time! If I could hang you all on the instant, believe me, I would. And I would be justified. This is rebellion against your own Provincial Congress. Have you seen the damage?"

"Yes, and it doesn't come to much at all. Nor was anyone, I believe, so much as wounded."

He shook his finger violently at me for a moment, too angry to talk.

"Now listen. I am determined to keep Tryon right here in our midst. And unharmed. He is our only shield against future real cannonading. And I intend to have your cooperation in achieving this. I am asking for a meeting with the Sons committee this morning and I want your influence among them to help me. In fact, this is an ultimatum: cease your activities against Tryon at once or cease forthwith to see Elisabeth and give up all hope in her direction."

He stopped and drew himself up. "Now you have it plain. And I mean every syllable. If necessary I'll order a ship readied at once to take her to the West Indies."

From my innermost core came my reply. "As far as I am concerned, Tryon, the English, and the entire Old World must go."

He set his lips and in a mute rage conducted me to the door.

As I came out on the street I saw people running—militia, children, oldsters. I marveled idly that life in our city was becoming one excitement after another.

I caught a passing militiaman by the arm. "What's happening?"

And when he told me I laughed. Mirthless laughter, but laughter it was, breaking out of me through the wall of my anger.

I ran with the others a block to the waterfront and saw with my own eyes—then ran back to the Kluger house and pounded on the door till I was let in.

I found Kluger still in the sitting room—and now

Elisabeth was with him, a bouquet of freshly cut flowers on her arm showing me where she had been earlier.

Kluger looked coldly determined. Elisabeth's eyes were ablaze. At my entry she uttered a cry, and running across the room she circled me with her arms.

"You've come to change your reply?" Kluger said.

"Nothing of the sort. I've come to tell you you're fighting yesterday's battle. Your precious governor is running away."

"No!"

"Oh, yes. Bag and baggage he's packing himself off to the ships. You can see for yourself if you like. Any window that gives on the harbor will show you."

Kluger's mouth opened but nothing came out. He rushed from the room and we followed after him to another chamber which gave a view southward.

Out on the water, halfway to the *Duchess of Gordon*, labored a barge freighted with bundles and boxes and furniture, and crowded with William Tryon and his recently landed official family. And ringing the harborside, watching, was a jeering, hooting, laughing crowd.

"Damme!" exclaimed Kluger. "The man hasn't the courage of a gnat. He's frightened to death of what he imagines will be the response to his warship's few cannon-balls. They'll really bombard, now."

"Never," I said. "Last night's few shots were a mistake committed by some angry subordinate officer. The firing ceased at once. The British know as well as we do that this is the best harbor in North America. They fondly imagine they'll invest us and fight the war comfortably from here. They haven't the least intention of smashing the place down."

Kluger glared at me.

"Come," I said to Elisabeth, "let's hurry along. It will be a pity to miss seeing the last of the royal governor."

"You'll stay right here, Elisabeth," Kluger pronounced. "You're to have nothing to do with this madman henceforth. And if you find it too difficult to abide by my injunction a visit with your Uncle Joseph in the West Indies may help. And you, sir," he said to me, "you are not welcome in this house, now, nor at any time hereafter."

17.

January 1776

ALL THROUGH THE NIGHT I sat at my table and read over and over again a single pamphlet of some eighty pages.

While the stars wheeled slowly across the blue-black sky, and until the inky surface of the East River lightened to gray, I absorbed the most marvelous piece of political writing I had ever seen.

" 'Tis not the affair of a City, a County or a Kingdom; but of a Continent. . . . Posterity are virtually involved in the contest and will be more or less affected to the end of time. . . ."

Driving arguments followed, couched in wonderfully lucid terms, illuminating most truly the fundamental issues of the struggle and making clear their meaning for the life of every ordinary man, woman, and child in America.

And all was shaped into a clarion call for revolution and independence: "O! Ye that love mankind! Ye that dare oppose not only the tyranny but the tyrant, stand forth! Every spot of the old world is overrun with oppression. Freedom hath been hunted round the globe. . . . O! receive the fugitive and prepare in time an asylum for mankind."

I marveled and mused, thrilled by the author's vision of a free, democratic republic of the future. Only a spirit itself on fire could fashion so effective a propaganda flame. And yet, among the other remarkable things about this pamphlet was the fact that its author, genius though he must be, was not named. "Common Sense," the work was titled, but the author signed himself only "An Englishman." I was familiar with the style of every major pamphleteer in the colonies and could identify them all regardless of which of their various pseudonyms they employed, yet I had never before seen a word from this pen.

We must reprint this pamphlet by the thousands, I determined—by the tens of thousands—and give it away free. Who, after reading it, would not zealously throw himself into the patriot cause! I would propose the printing at this afternoon's meeting of the Sons, where we were to consider the latest step backward of the merchants.

For, astonishingly enough, Kluger and the conservative merchants had found a way to retain the link with Tryon and England.

They had the necessary votes in the colony-wide Provincial Congress, and with these they appointed a committee which went out to the British warships and negotiated an agreement. We would supply Tryon and His Majesty's ships with their necessary provisions, if, in return, the ships refrained from bombarding the town.

And Tryon could continue to consider himself governor of New York, even though it would be the better part of valor for him to stay aboard his ship.

Ostensibly, the merchants had saved the city from destruction. In this wise they justified their action to the populace. In truth, they had, and quite cunningly, managed to hold onto their beloved legal relationship with Great Britain, and to their way back, whenever it became possible, to the old order and its feudal protections against "mobocracy."

The Sons could think of no riposte. Tryon himself was safely beyond our reach. And in the Provincial Congress, the conservative faction held the majority.

When General Washington sent us his second in command to help prepare New York against a possible British assault, which in the minds of the military men had now become an imminent possibility, that officer found us in this ridiculous circumstance.

On taking up his quarters among us, General Charles Lee sent a note to the Provincial Congress asking that representatives meet with him to discuss strategy for defending the city, and that billeting arrangements be made for the fifteen hundred troops of the advance guard which would soon arrive from Boston.

Consternation seized the conservative majority of the Provincial Congress. All the fears about armed conflict that might make the breach with England irreparable sprang into highest relief. They appointed a delegation so uncooperative in its outlook that on second thought they decided to add several of the Sons to it, even if only for the sake of appearances.

The following morning, at nine o'clock, we waited on the general in the drawing room of the De Vries house.

Three-quarters of an hour after we arrived an aide entered to tell us the general was ready to receive us—in his bedroom. He had just finished breakfast.

We glanced round at one another and followed the aide

upstairs. There, in a wide canopied bed, lay General Charles Lee, propped up against the pillows and fondling the muzzle of a huge hound which stood with its forepaws on the bed. Some three or four other dogs, equally huge, lolled about the room.

"Ah, there, gentlemen, happy to see you. Come in, come in, please, and seat yourselves—right here on the bed. That will be best. Those of you who can't find room may stand close. I like my conferences close up. Makes for quickness. Otherwise the business gets out of hand and it all becomes a bore."

The general spoke in a high-pitched voice, thin almost to querulousness, but rapid, and with a very clipped English accent. He had a small, round head with protruding, round eyes, a large nose, and a sharply receding chin, so that at first glance he seemed strangely like an angry and upset child.

He had a great reputation in Europe, however, as a professional soldier, and the Continental Congress had been glad to avail itself of his experience when he had offered his services.

"Go away, now, Caesar," he said to the dog on the bed, pushing him aside; but the dog insisted on remaining and would budge only his massive head with the general's shove. "Oh, well, to business, gentlemen." And so it was that the delegation members closest to Caesar had to keep one wary eye on that dog's whims.

"I am here as the advance guard of the Continental Army, gentlemen; and much is to be done, very much, and that with the utmost speed. Our aim, to tell it to you in a word, is to defend your city against the oncoming enemy. Our problem lies in the fact that the city is indefensible."

166

We stared at him, as much taken by the novelty of his personality as by the significance of his news.

"Come, gentlemen, wake up, I beg you! You look like so many abandoned puppets. Henry!" he screamed suddenly in a tone that pierced the entire house. And in ran an aide, a slovenly dressed, harassed-looking soldier wearing the insignia of a captain. "Bring me the map from that table—the very biggest map."

"You see, gentlemen," he went on, "real soldiers do not defend cities that cannot be defended, but in this war we appear to be burdened with an additional consideration— the citizen and his confounded morale. Feelings would be hurt, they tell me, if we did the proper thing and abandoned your city to obviously superior forces. So we are going to expend a part of our already insufficient ordnance and several thousand lives to make the citizenry feel better before we withdraw."

Then, to Henry the aide, who now approached with a large, unfolded map, "High time, fool! No, Caesar." The dog had snapped at the dangling lower edge of the map, but the general, with surprising agility, pulled it instantly beyond his reach.

"Now, then, gentlemen, you see your city." His hand and mouth expressed an apologetic deprecation, as though he were displaying a decaying fruit. "It begins at the south, here, on a great bay, open to the guns of any and all warships—of which the enemy has all and we haven't any." He giggled suddenly at his quip. "And now it continues northward between two rivers to become a long, thin island, each river navigable to the largest ships of war, which means that if we station an army on this island, as we intend to do, it can be cut off and surrounded by landings from these warships wherever and however the enemy chooses. I have been directed to overcome this somewhat by taking a further step in the direction of suicide: part of our army will be encamped here on Brooklyn Heights, on the other side of the East River, so that we will not be destroyed all at one blow—and also, so that whatever chance a unified army might have had of extricating itself is now lost by the division into two weaker halves with a broad river between them."

He looked up, his face radiating extreme energy—almost, I had the momentary sense, akin to madness. "Do you understand, gentlemen?" he shouted at us.

And before anyone could make a response his round little eyes filled with hatred and a most shocking glare possessed his face. "And this is the problem I have been given to work with! This is what the Continental Congress and its commander-in-chief insist I turn into a victory that will bring the war to a smashing, swift conclusion. Do you understand?"

He was fairly screaming now. We of the delegation knew not where to look—whether at one another or at him.

His voice dropped, and he spoke in a new tone, low and vibrating with passion of a most determined sort.

"But defend the city we shall, gentlemen, believe me. And even with some real possibility of success. For we shall turn the city itself into a battlefield. We shall dig trenches in every main thoroughfare and ditches in every street, and we shall throw up barricades at every crossing and make a fort of every structure. If the enemy does succeed in taking the city, he will succeed in nothing else thereafter, so costly will we have made the victory. Do you follow me, gentlemen?"

Indeed we did. His meaning was unmistakable. Even the hounds were following him.

"Splendid. Our conference is almost over. Of you I will require two things: organization of your inhabitants so that the trenches will be dug and the redoubts thrown up as I and my staff will indicate; and billeting arrangements for the Continental Army, which will arrive here so soon as the enemy evacuates Boston—which we have reason to believe will take place shortly. I am pleased to have met you, gentlemen. Kindly leave a list of your names with Henry and an indication of where I may send for you, as I need."

And Henry was ushering us out.

Just as we reached the door, the thin, harsh voice, so close to being a scream, rose at us once more.

"Oh, yes, a final word. About that blackguard Tryon. All communication with him is to cease at once, as is this nonsense of supplying him with provisions."

This horrified the conservative delegates. "Sever the governor's supplies! Why, we can't possibly! At least, not yet. We would first have to—"

"I will hang whoever offers that spy so much as a cup of water. As of today, the rogue may forage for his supplies in England. Mark me, gentlemen, this is a command. Good morning to you."

18.

THE AFTERNOON of that same day Brigadier General Alexander MacDougall and Major Jamie Hardy of the New York militia had another interview with General Lee.

The general was acquainting himself with the resources of the city. And though his disdain deepened observably to disgust as we explained to him whence our rank and the nature of the troops we commanded, his protruding eyes concentrated with attention as we enlightened him on the city's politics: that the conservative merchants were interested in saving their money and their skins, unlike the merchants of Boston, whereas the Sons and their followers had considered themselves at war with England this year past.

At last he understood that we of the Sons of Liberty were offering him our devoted service without stint and without measure.

"Capital!" he cried, striking his hands together. "Come, now, pay attention."

He was still wearing his nightclothes, as in the morning interview, but now he threw a tunic over them, and dropping to his hands and knees he began scrambling about on the floor among maps and charts. Brows knit, thinking hard, talking to himself, he motioned us to come down also. As he moved among the maps he asked questions—the widths of streets, depths of various declivities, heights of churches and warehouses.

It became apparent that our information was being used by a mind that could boast a confident grasp of the techniques of warfare. After pauses for deliberation, and with sharp nods to himself, he marked signs upon the maps clearly and forcefully.

The army was to be divided into sections, as he had already told us, one to be stationed on Manhattan and another on Brooklyn Heights; and in front of these, the city itself was to constitute a great honeycomb of defenses manned by a third force. The success of the action was to be measured by how much it cost the enemy to win the city street by street.

After some four hours of unflagging application, we emerged, heartened beyond measure by what seemed a most workable plan for dealing the enemy a severe blow.

And then we fell to.

Under the direction of the Sons and our militia, the sounds of the shovel and the pick, the hammer and the saw, the crowbar and the axe now spread through the city in a clanking, rattling, knocking cacophony. Every soldier and citizen devoted to the patriot cause strove to realize the diagrams drawn by General Lee and his staff, improving upon the details with ingenious additions.

The face of the city was transformed. Parapets, embankments, barriers, and ditches appeared amidst a welter of raw earth, felled trees, and cobblestones. At the end of each major street that led to the rivers a cannon was mounted, with an embankment thrown up before it for the protection of the cannoneers, and breastworks behind for their defense from within the city. And farther in, each street was barricaded, the earth piled high between loose walls of cobblestones.

At the Battery, the north wall of Fort George, abandoned now by the British, who had all taken to their ships in the harbor, was ripped away so that the structure could not be used as a citadel by a force capturing it from the bay. And, rather devilishly, a traverse had been erected on the Bowling Green beyond it, in order that the exposed interior could be swept by cannon fire, making a vast trap out of the shell for any such seaborne capturers.

A little north of the traverse, across the entrance to Broadway, a great earth and tree trunk barrier, fully a story high, was thrown up; and across many of the other streets monstrously high man-made ridges were similarly placed so that the town could not easily be swept by enemy cannon fire. Within the subdivisions created by these structures numerous smaller breastworks were erected. The town resembled a huge grid of parapets and ditches studded at many of the street corners with forts composed of tree trunks or cobblestones.

Amidst this network swarmed two types of humanity: soldiers, most wearing the colors and uniforms of the various Continental Army regiments which arrived each day from the north, and some, from our own militia, without uniforms; and citizenry, fleeing from the city.

For it was coming home to all that here the American high command proposed to make a stand; and great

172

numbers elected to get out of the way. With bedding strapped on their shoulders and dog carts overloaded with furniture and pots and pans, streams of people made their way, day after day, over and around the barriers, some aiming northward, for Connecticut, others westward, hoping to get to New Jersey by way of the ferry crossings.

And now came the news that the British were evacuating Boston. Besieged by an American army that had grown to twenty thousand, they awoke one morning to find themselves, in addition, staring up at two hundred cannon that had been captured at Ticonderoga. And so, embarking upon a huge war fleet, the enemy was expected to try for the more advantageous prize of New York.

Every day contingents of the Continental Army arrived, dispatched with haste from around Boston. On a crisp afternoon in late March a thousand soldiers marched into the city, led by General Israel Putnam. The very next day a brigade of five thousand New Englanders, under General Heath, sailed into Turtle Bay. We had scarce managed to designate landing places for all their vessels when General John Sullivan arrived through the Hell Gate passage with six additional regiments floated on twenty-three more transports. And behind him came General Nathaniel Greene with another brigade of five thousand men.

Night and day we galloped the roads on the upper island and on Brooklyn Heights, guiding regiments and other units to encampments, and offering our knowledge of the terrain for the organization of supply and communication lines.

General Washington himself, commanding the last of the arrivals from Boston, entered the city. Our hearts rose. We

173

no longer doubted that we had the strength to smash the British whenever they should oblige us by putting in an appearance.

And, after a delay for refitting at Halifax, they did.

One day came the ominous information that a gigantic British war fleet had been sighted moving toward New York.

Two days later I stood on the high ground at Sandy Hook with delegates to the Provincial Congress and others and watched the warships coming in.

All day long we stood and observed while ship after ship negotiated the bar. From a forest of masts that spread across the horizon out on the Atlantic one ship after another detached itself, made for the channel, came across the lip, and entered the great lower bay to sail unhindered far up and cast anchor.

The skies were perfect, the east wind favoring; and without mishap, and seemingly without end, the men-of-war followed one another in single file till the skyline of the lower bay, vast as it was—almost an inland sea—was dark with masts.

They must have borne a hundred times the number of cannon in all of New York. My assurance gave way to defiance, and by afternoon to a dogged determination.

"No need to overestimate them simply because you see all their strength gathered together before your eyes," said MacDougall. He had guessed my thoughts. "If you saw all our own forces on parade before you it would come to much the same thing."

The portents of approaching battle reminded MacDougall of other days. "I fought on their side on the seas in the last war, y'know—commanded a privateer. Their guns are good but the ships are rotten, and what's worse, the men have no stomach for fight. They're poor devils who've been kidnapped off the streets and beaten and starved for discipline. A squad of our men will do for a company of theirs, believe me."

Yet we were a sober group when we turned our horses northward for the ride back to New York.

19.

THE MEETING CHAMBER was filled. Almost everyone was present, yet we remained a tiny legislature as the world's assemblies have gone. Some thirty-odd of us in the Provincial Congress represented all the counties in the province, and of these only twenty were needed to constitute a quorum.

It was both exciting and strange to think that this small group had a hand on the tiller that steered the destiny of a continent.

We used high-backed chairs arranged in several loose rows before the chairman's table, and we changed our seats from meeting to meeting as the spirit moved us. Kluger, too, was here, and as usual he ignored my existence.

Doctor Weston of the Presbyterian church said a prayer, the minutes of the previous meeting were read, and then Henry Remsen, in the chair, announced the business of the session.

"We have had a communication from our delegates at Philadelphia explaining the momentous matter which has been placed before the Continental Congress and asking instructions from this body as to how they should cast their vote.

"You are all by now acquainted with the contents of that communication and I believe we may proceed directly to the question."

Whereupon Alexander MacDougall offered the motion, "Resolved that this body instruct its delegates at the Continental Congress to vote affirmatively on the question of creating from these colonies an independent nation."

I seconded the motion and the debate opened.

At once there erupted all the anger and exasperation of the conservatives at being pulled willy-nilly along the road to rebellion. Likewise, there flared all the frustration of the Sons of Liberty, who saw the colonies engaged in a war in every sense except the name and still lacking what was to us the only justifiable objective—independence.

"We are in actual and undeniable fact already at war," argued Alexander MacDougall. "Bunker Hill, Ticonderoga, Boston, the existence of a central government of our own at Philadelphia and of a continent-wide army to support it all prove that. It is the wildest folly not to declare openly that independence is our aim and thus release to the full the enthusiasm and energies of the people."

"No, sir," replied a spokesman of the merchants. "We are in dire disagreement with the king and Parliament, true enough, and armed clashes have broken out here and there, but to call this a war is surely willful exaggeration. There is no war in progress as yet, thank God, and it is the duty of all men of wisdom and forbearance to avert one. Surely, to declare that independence is our goal is to commit ourselves to the devastation of our own land and to eventual defeat. Why, who here imagines we can withstand the cannon of the fleet which arrived yesterday? Or the thirty thousand men in that fleet? The entire force mustered to defend this city at this very moment can not be more than twenty thousand. We have won a victory at Boston, a bloodless one. Can we not wait to see what bearing this has on negotiations?"

"You cruelly twist the military facts," answered Mac-Dougall, "and the military situation is becoming the central consideration. Most probably the united colonies by themselves could cope with the forces Britain is able to send against us. But consider France. All the world knows the French are straining for the opportunity to throw in men, gold, and ships on our side—to strike back at England for the loss of Canada, to open trade with the American continent from which England keeps her shut out. The French only await a signal from us that we are sincere—that we mean to separate—for, of course, they will not risk a war and its cost merely to help us make up our differences with Britain. A declaration that we fight for our freedom would guarantee us France's help, and victory."

John Alsop rose and deflected the discussion from that channel.

"Still, one certainty remains, stark and grim: whether or no we won out eventually in a war of independence, this city would be destroyed. Not a home would remain standing. Not a warehouse or wharf. And all our property would be forfeit. Every aspect of this city's uniquely dangerous position cries out that we be circumspect and, for the moment at least, abjure declarations of war."

I took the floor.

"The vote today will be a critical one in our history—critical, I believe, to the history of all mankind. And I, for one, cannot abide it that at such a juncture the vital issues should be obscured in talk which devolves upon secondary considerations.

"Gentlemen, your fear is not the king and Parliament, nor the number of British ships and soldiers. For it is plain military fact, quite as General MacDougall has just said, that were we to declare our aim is independence and thereby achieve the support of France, the military victory would be assured.

"No, gentlemen, the cause of your fear lies elsewhere. What you truly fear is democracy—'mobocracy,' as some of you put it with so much clever distaste. It is fear of what the victory for independence may bring us here at home."

There were no cries of protest as I paused for breath. Rather, the delegates watched me intently—some defiantly, some angrily, some even nodding agreement and meaning by it that they felt themselves quite justified in their fear.

"The real question in your minds is: Shall we submit to Parliament and be robbed to a certain extent, or shall we face the dangers of a new nation in which every drayman and every water seller may help make the laws and so endanger our property to an extent unknown?

"Gentlemen, there is no need to fear the people who make up a nation if only you are willing to allow them their part in the great potential wealth of this continent. Let them but have the farms they are entitled to, and, in the cities, the decent considerations which are their due, and you will make of them as ardent respecters and defenders of property as any who have amassed ships and lands and plate.

"The real difficulty lies inside yourselves. Is your aim to engross all, after the example of the lords of England? Then

179

you have good cause to fear, and to look for protection to a government which rules tyrannically and with an iron fist.

"Or can you bring yourselves to accept the self-interest of others—of the people at large?

"If you can, an entire community may go forward on this continent toward a destiny the world has often dreamed of, but never yet seen. This will be the meaning of your vote here, today."

With that I sat down.

Alexander MacDougall rose and said quietly, "Our young colleague has put the case as clearly as we can hope to have it presented. We are content to bring the question to a vote."

Nevertheless, when the voting was completed, the resolution to instruct the New York delegates to vote for independence was decisively defeated.

20.

July 1776

STRAIGHT-BACKED AND SLIM, she sat quietly in the center of the sofa. Composed, yet alert, her dark eyes radiating an intensity that belied her outer calm, she affected me so strangely after our brief separation that for a moment I couldn't speak.

"Oh, I was so glad to see Tommy, and to get your note! Oh, Jamie!"

I sat down beside her, and putting my arm around her waist, drew her close.

Tears wet her cheeks. She gently pushed me away. "We must be quick. I don't know when my father will be back. If he finds you here he *will* send me to the West Indies, and we might really never again see each other."

"I felt I had to risk it," I said. "We've been mustered into the Continental Army and must go now wherever we're ordered. And at any moment the British may make their opening move. They need only for the wind to veer into a favoring quarter—and after that no one can foretell events."

"Oh, Jamie, if a war really begins—will it be a long one?"

181

"Not if we crush them here in New York. It will be brief. But if we lose here—"

"Oh, Jamie!"

"Yes. That's why I've come. Where the Continental Army would go after that, and how long the fighting would last—and what might happen to me—that can't be foreseen."

"Jamie!"

"I had to come, no matter what the risk, to ask you, Elisabeth: Will you consider yourself engaged to me?"

"Yes, I will. I do, Jamie, yes!"

We embraced again. I took from my pocket a plain narrow gold band, with a tiny ruby set in it. "Mistress Rowe of the Spread Sail gave it to me. She said it was my mother's and was to go to the woman I married."

"I daren't wear it openly," she whispered, "but I'll carry it with me always."

"Till the war ends. Till I come home."

"Yes."

We held each other again. Then a sharp sound somewhere in the house startled us and we drew apart.

"The Provincial Congress session should be about over and your father may be back shortly. I'll manage to see you again, soon, no matter what."

"Oh, Jamie, Jamie, do take care of yourself."

With a final kiss I said goodbye and slipped out of the room and through the garden door.

I strode along, only gradually becoming aware of the pandemonium around me. On all sides there was drumming, as on that wonderful morning after the news that Boston had dumped the tea.

"By heaven, it cannot be—" I exclaimed out loud. I caught a dancing soldier by the arm. "What is it, man?"

"What is it? Why, we've become an independent nation! The Congress at Philadelphia has just declared it so! Here, Major, here's a torch for you. Or would you rather have something wet? The tavern keepers are serving free to all soldiers, God bless 'em."

I let go his arm and he was swept along with the crowd. Crazily swaying effigies of King George and Lord North with ropes dangling from their necks wobbled past me, and I saw a great placard with Franklin's famous drawing of the colonies in the form of a snake cut into parts, the motto "Unite or Perish" beneath. The fifes screamed "Yankee Doodle" as though it had never been really played before.

So it had come to pass! Without the consent of New York, but a declaration of independence nevertheless. And in the nature of things, now binding on all!

The meaning of it welled into my feelings. I stepped back out of the path of the parades and leaned against a railing, suddenly slack with the fulfillment of two years of striving, my eyes smarting with gratitude to whatever fate rules matters.

Another procession came merrily along the street. I followed in its wake to the center of our small world, the Common, and there I pressed my way through the crowds to Hampden Hall to stand with my back to the old meeting house.

On the public grounds before the Liberty Pole tumultuous thousands were gathering. All the spontaneous parades throughout the town and all the celebrators assembled in a great free and easy intermingling.

Excited orators, lifted onto the shoulders of friends, urged on those around them; torches waved by the hundreds; flimsy gallows rose to the accompaniment of cheers and laughter; slogans chanted by small groups were caught up in widening circles till hundreds were calling them; and through and above all the fifes played and the drums reverberated.

Amid the great commotion criers made their way announcing that later that day, toward evening, the troops would be drawn up upon the Common at the order of General Washington to hear a solemn reading of the Declaration of Independence.

I disengaged myself from the jubilant throngs. We would organize one final great parade, a victory parade, and as the streets were all barricaded now, march round and round the Common.

21.

THE LATE AFTERNOON SUN shone down on a scene more magnificent and solemn than any we had ever before witnessed.

Virtually the entire town was assembled at the Common, where colorful, massed ranks of soldiers formed a great square, cannoneer companies lined up on one side, cavalry opposite them, and foot soldiers on the other two sides. Outside the square crowded the civilian population, overflowing into the surrounding streets and filling the avenues that led into the area.

Within the military square, facing a line of drummer boys, stood a tier of seats set up for the members of the Provincial Congress. As I waited at one end of the tier to mount and take a seat Martin Kluger approached with Elisabeth on his arm.

For an instant I did not know what to say in greeting, or whether I should greet him at all. But Kluger put out his hand to be shaken.

"We are all in the same ship for a certainty, now, Jamie," he said.

"Yes, sir, we are," I replied.

"Won't you sit with us?" he asked. "I've brought Elisabeth along to view the proceedings from the Congress seats."

I followed them up the little set of steps and along the line of chairs and we sat down together, Elisabeth between Kluger and myself. Something in Kluger's manner gave me the impression that he knew everything about us and accepted the state of affairs. And the instant we were seated my guess was confirmed.

Leaning across Elisabeth, he said, "Jamie, I'm relieved that you and Elisabeth have decided of your own to defer your marriage till the war is over. A prudent father could want no less."

"We're glad you agree, sir," I said, taking Elisabeth's hand.

He nodded soberly and reflectively.

Elisabeth gave her father a quick kiss, and when she turned to smile at me her eyes were shining.

The line of drummers executed a long, thunderous roll, and through an opening in the ranks of soldiery, General Washington rode slowly into the square, with some fifteen or twenty of his staff. They ranged themselves behind the drummers, the general on a white charger in the center of their line. From one end of the line, while the drums continued rolling, a crier with a scroll rode forward and took up a position in front of all. Still mounted, he opened his scroll. The drumming ceased.

"Hear ye, hear ye, hear ye!" he called. "By order of General Washington, commanding the troops of these free and independent states—" mighty cheers arose on all sides at the words "free" and "independent"—"I shall read out

186

the Declaration of Independence proclaimed by the Continental Congress of these states."

Another roll of the drums ensued, creating a solemn punctuation. The crier began to read.

" 'When in the course of human events it becomes necessary for one people to dissolve the political bands which have connected them with another, and to assume among the powers of the earth the separate and equal station to which the laws of Nature and of Nature's God entitle them, a decent respect to the opinions of mankind requires that they should declare the causes which impel them to the separation.' "

I was pleased by the statesmanlike tone of the opening theme, and agreeably surprised at the literary polish with which the argument was presented.

" 'We hold these truths to be self-evident: that all men are created equal, that they are endowed by their Creator with certain unalienable rights, that among these are life, liberty, and the pursuit of happiness. That to secure these rights, governments are instituted among men, deriving their just powers from the consent of the governed—' "

My admiration turned to wonder. How marvelous that these as yet emerging concepts should already be expressed in a document of state—should be accepted as the goals of a government!

I looked around excitedly at the sea of faces. I wished I could seize every man by the coat and say to him, "Listen most carefully, absorb every syllable. It is your birthright you are hearing, brought to you openly and clearly for the first time. If the British win this war, perhaps it will not be brought to you again in your lifetime. So carry away in your memory every iota."

I listened intently. A world of the most advanced, the most humane political philosophy was being expounded.

" '. . . that whenever any form of government becomes destructive of these ends, it is the right of the people to alter or to abolish it. . . . Prudence, indeed, will dictate that governments long established should not be changed for light and transient causes. . . . But when a long train of abuses and usurpations, pursuing invariably the same object, evinces a design to reduce them under absolute despotism, it is their right, it is their duty, to throw off such government.' "

Now came a marshaling of our complaints against England showing the intention to establish and maintain such a destructive despotism.

Then the crier's voice rose even higher and more affirmatively than before.

" 'We, therefore, the representatives of the United States of America, in general congress, assembled, appealing to the Supreme Judge of the World for the rectitude of our intentions, do, in the name, and by the authority of the good people of these colonies, solemnly publish and declare, that these united colonies are, and of right ought to be, free and independent states—' "

Cheering broke out, wild and full, a great celebration all in itself, filling the Common and echoing to the skies. The crier waited, patiently and long, till it began to subside.

" '. . . that they are absolved from all allegiance to the British Crown, and that all political connection between them and the State of Great Britain, is and ought to be totally dissolved; and that as free and independent states, they have full power to levy war, conclude peace, contract alliances, establish commerce, and to do all other acts and things which independent states may of right do.' "

Again cheering broke out and the crier waited. Then, in a more measured pace, signaling the end, he read out, " 'And for the support of this declaration, with a firm reliance on the protection of divine Providence, we mutually pledge to each other our lives, our fortunes, and our sacred honor.'"

In the moment of silence before the cheering rose again I sat riveted by the effect. In the midst of the tumult that followed, I was engulfed by a sense of the communion of all the souls embarked on this adventure.

The drums began to roll, along with the cheering. Salute after salute was fired from the cannon at the end of the Common.

Then, orders for the troops to march out began to be called. With their drums and fifes playing, one after another the units faced off and moved away.

And as the formal ceremony dissolved, the town resumed its wild celebration.

The three of us, Elisabeth, Kluger, and myself, made our way together off the Common to walk to the Kluger house. For some unaccountable reason we found ourselves in the very heart of the dispersing multitude. Everyone else seemed to be hastening in the same direction.

Just then Kluger turned and glanced upward. I followed his look. He was gazing at the long, thin pennant which flew from the Liberty Pole against the early evening sky. It stood out stiffly now in a fresh southerly breeze.

"I know your thoughts," I said. "The British fleet may well hoist sail in such a wind and move in."

"Just so. The issue will be joined very shortly, Jamie."

We arrived at the Bowling Green in company, it seemed, with almost the entire confluence which had just massed on the Common. And then we saw what the attraction was.

In the center of the little park stood the gilded leaden statue of George the Third proudly mounted on a horse. Around and about the statue a riotous crew was making preparations to tear it down. Two men had climbed up on the horse and were fixing ropes around the neck of the king and around the horse's body. Below them waited others with axes in their hands. At every motion, whether successful or inept, the growing, gleeful crowd roared and clapped and shouted advice.

We stopped and watched. At last the ropes were secured. To the applause of the crowd the men slid down. Those with axes began to chop away at the horse's feet. In the time it took to make ten or twelve cuts the whole royal configuration began to give and tip. With a mighty and satisfying crash it came tumbling over on its side.

The axemen leapt upon it, chopping the leaden limbs asunder while the crowd shouted, "Bullets for the Continental Army! That's the way we'll send it back to them!"

Unable to contain themselves longer, the onlookers swarmed onto the green, dodging about amongst the falling axes and snatching up the pieces. A new parade formed, and they were off again to the Common to exhibit the spoils.

I looked at Kluger. His expression was heavy.

"At bottom," I said to him, "you fear them."

"Perhaps. Perhaps not. It's no longer so easy for me to say as it was a year ago. Then I'd have said, 'Of course!' "

"They're only celebrating the achievement of their goal," I said. "They don't know how to do it maturely, yet. But they'll learn. Especially if the mandates of the declaration we've just heard are really and truly put into practice."

He smiled suddenly and warmly. "By Heaven, Jamie, your faith is most moving. I do believe some little bit of it is rubbing off on me. Well, let's get this war over with, now that it's here, and then we'll see."

I understood that he found himself on the threshold of a whole new world of beliefs. I took his hand and shook it to welcome him across. With my other arm I circled Elisabeth; and I knew that all for which it is worth staking one's life was mine.

ABOUT THE AUTHOR

Leon Solomon White brings to his first novel for young people the qualifications of journalist, soldier, historian, and now, staff member of the American History Division of the New York Public Library. Convinced that American history as it is all too often taught is a lifeless tableau of patriotic pieties, he has attempted to present dramatically and understandably how we have coped—successfully and unsuccessfully—with the real and important issues and crises that are our experience as a people. Mr. White lives with his family in Bayside, New York.